BEATITUDES

RANIERO CANTALAMESSA, O.F.M. CAP

Blessed are the poor in spirit, for theirs is the kingdom of heaven. Blessed are they who mourn, for they shall be comforted. Blessed are the meek, for they shall inherit the earth. Blessed are they who hunger and thirst for righteousness, for they shall be satisfied. Blessed are the merciful, for they shall obtain mercy. Blessed are the pure of heart, for they shall see God. Blessed are the peacemakers, for they shall be called children of God. Blessed are they who are persecuted for the sake of righteousness, for theirs is the kingdom of heaven.

beatitudes

EIGHT

STEPS

TO

happiness

TRANSLATED BY MARSHA DAIGLE-WILLIAMSON, PH.D.

SERVANT
BOOKS

PUBLISHED BY ST. ANTHONY MESSENGER PRESS
CINCINNATI, OHIO

Cover and book design by Mark Sullivan
Cover image copyright © Design Pics/Don Hammond

LIBRARY OF CONGRESS CATALOGING-IN-PUBLICATION DATA
Cantalamessa, Raniero.
[Beatitudini evangeliche. English]
Beatitudes : eight steps to happiness / Raniero Cantalamessa ; translated by Marsha Daigle-Williamson.
p. cm.
Includes bibliographical references and index.
ISBN 978-0-86716-922-5 (pbk. : alk. paper) 1. Beatitudes. 2. Happiness—Religious aspects—Christianity. I. Title.
BT382.C3613 2009
226.9'3—dc22
2009031555

ISBN 978-0-86716-922-5

First published in Italian under the title *Le beatitudini evangeliche. Otto gradini verso la felicità*, Edizioni San Paolo, 2008.

Published by Servant Books, an imprint of St. Anthony Messenger Press.
28 W. Liberty St.
Cincinnati, OH 45202
www.ServantBooks.org

Printed in the United States of America.

Printed on acid-free paper.

10 11 12 13 5 4 3 2

Contents

PREFACE | *ix*

THE BEATITUDES: MATTHEW AND LUKE | *xi*

CHAPTER ONE

BLESSED ARE THE POOR IN SPIRIT, FOR THEIRS IS THE KINGDOM OF
HEAVEN

· *The Poor and the Poor in Spirit* | *1*

· *The Theological Explanation Is Insufficient* | *3*

· *Poverty in Christ's Life* | *6*

· *To Be for the Poor and to Be Poor* | *10*

· *Why Voluntary Poverty?* | *14*

· *The Contemporary Relevance of the Beatitude on Poverty* | *16*

CHAPTER TWO

BLESSED ARE YOU THAT WEEP NOW, FOR YOU SHALL LAUGH

· *A New Relationship Between Pleasure and Pain* | *20*

· *Where Is Your God?* | *24*

· *"Let the Priests, the Ministers of the Lord, Weep"* | *28*

· *The Best Tears* | *30*

CHAPTER THREE

BLESSED ARE THE MEEK, FOR THEY SHALL INHERIT THE EARTH

· *Two Keys to Reading the Beatitudes* | *34*

· *Jesus, the Meek One* | *37*

· *Meekness and Tolerance* | *39*

· *With Meekness and Reverence* | *42*

· *Learn From Me, for I Am Meek* | *43*

· *Putting on the Meekness of Christ* | *47*

CHAPTER FOUR

BLESSED ARE YOU WHO HUNGER NOW, FOR YOU SHALL BE SATISFIED

· *History and Spirit* | 49

· *Who Are the Hungry and the Satisfied?* | 51

· *A Contemporary Parable* | 56

· *"Blessed Are Those Who Hunger and Thirst for Righteousness"* | 58

· *Physical Bread and Eucharistic Bread* | 61

CHAPTER FIVE

BLESSED ARE THE MERCIFUL, FOR THEY SHALL OBTAIN MERCY

· *The Mercy of Christ* | 65

· *A God Who Delights in Showing Mercy* | 67

· *Our Mercy: Cause or Effect of God's Mercy?* | 70

· *Experiencing Divine Mercy* | 72

· *A Church "Rich in Mercy"* | 74

· *"Put on...Compassion"* | 75

CHAPTER SIX

BLESSED ARE THE PURE IN HEART, FOR THEY SHALL SEE GOD

· *From Ritual Purity to Purity of Heart* | 79

· *A Look at History* | 83

· *We Have Two Lives* | 86

· *One Kind of Collective Hypocrisy* | 89

· *Religious Hypocrisy* | 92

CHAPTER SEVEN

BLESSED ARE THE PEACEMAKERS, FOR THEY SHALL BE CALLED
    SONS OF GOD

· *Who Are the Peacemakers?* | 97

· *The Message for World Day of Peace* | 99

· *Peace as a Gift* | 101

· *Peace as a Task: Religious Peace* | *104*

· *Peace Without Religion?* | *107*

CHAPTER EIGHT

BLESSED ARE THOSE WHO ARE PERSECUTED FOR RIGHTEOUSNESS'
SAKE, FOR THEIRS IS THE KINGDOM OF HEAVEN

· *Two Reasons for Persecution: Righteousness and the Name
of Christ* | *113*

· *Two Forms of Persecution: Death and Marginalization* | *115*

· *The Characteristics of a True Martyr: Love, Humility
and Grace* | *118*

· *Persecuted Unjustly or Justly?* | *124*

· *Before Descending the Mount* | *126*

APPENDIX

AN EXAMINATION OF CONSCIENCE BASED ON THE BEATITUDES | *133*

NOTES | *137*

Preface

This book is a collection of meditations on the Gospel beatitudes given to the papal household in the presence of Pope Benedict XVI during Advent of 2006 and Lent of 2007.

The beatitudes, even within the New Testament, underwent a development of different applications according to the theology of the particular Gospel writer and of the needs of the community for which he was writing. Exegetes have distinguished three successive phases in this process: the *initial phase*, consisting of the beatitudes as we assume they were originally formulated by Jesus during his life; the *intermediate phase*, represented by the oral traditions that preceded the writing of the Gospels, in which an initial interpretation was already underway; and the *last phase*, the final versions of the beatitudes that have reached us in the Gospels of Luke and Matthew, which are laid out in parallel following this preface. Jacques Dupont takes this approach in his monumental study on the beatitudes, and I will have an opportunity to present—and occasionally to discuss—his chief conclusions during the course of these meditations.

In keeping with the developing nature of applications for the beatitudes, we will also read the beatitudes in light of the new situations in which we find ourselves today, with the difference, of course, that the interpretations of the Gospel writers are inspired and are thus normative for everyone at all times, while today's interpretations do not share this special privilege.

What Saint Gregory the Great says of all of Scripture applies to the beatitudes as well, namely, "*Cum legentibus crescit*," "It grows with [the] persons reading...it."[1] Scripture always reveals new implications and richer content, according to the new needs and questions with which it is read. It is in this spirit that I intend to reflect on the beatitudes, attempting thereby to illumine our lives from the perspective of the beatitudes and to shed light on the beatitudes from our experiences.

According to Matthew, Jesus climbed a mountain in order to proclaim the beatitudes, and we will do the same to meditate on them. Each meditation will be like another step upward in the effort to scale this "eight-storey" mountain.

The Beatitudes

Matthew 5:3–12	Luke 6:20–26
Blessed are the poor in spirit, for theirs is the kingdom of heaven.	Blessed are you poor, for yours is the kingdom of God.
Blessed are those who mourn, for they shall be comforted.	Blessed are you that hunger now, for you shall be satisfied.
Blessed are the meek, for they shall inherit the earth.	Blessed are you that weep now, for you shall laugh.
Blessed are those who hunger and thirst for righteousness, for they shall be satisfied.	Blessed are you when men hate you, and when they exclude you and revile you, and cast out your name as evil, on account of the Son of man! Rejoice in that day, and leap for joy, for behold, your reward is great in heaven; for so their father did to the prophets.
Blessed are the merciful, for they shall obtain mercy.	
Blessed are the pure in heart, for they shall see God.	
	But woe to you that are rich, for you have received your consola- tion.
Blessed are the peacemakers, for they shall be called sons of God.	
Blessed are those who are perse- cuted for righteousness' sake, for theirs is the kingdom of heaven.	Woe to you that are full now, for you shall hunger.
	Woe to you that laugh now, for you shall mourn and weep.
Blessed are you when men revile you and persecute you and utter all kinds of evil against you falsely on my account. Rejoice and be glad, for your reward is great in heaven, for so men persecuted the prophets who were before you.	Woe to you, when all men speak well of you, for so their fathers did to the false prophets.

Chapter One

BLESSED ARE THE POOR IN SPIRIT, FOR THEIRS IS THE KINGDOM OF HEAVEN

The Poor and the Poor in Spirit

In regard to the first beatitude, there is first of all a literary problem: Matthew and Luke report the beatitudes to us in somewhat different ways. Matthew uses indirect discourse: "Blessed are the poor" (5:3); Luke uses direct address: "Blessed are you poor" (6:20). Matthew says, "The poor in spirit," while Luke simply says, "The poor."

The most plausible explanation seems to be that there is a common source that both Matthew and Luke depend on that simply said "poor." Luke, in his concern to emphasize the social significance of the word, keeps it as such and even reinforces it by contrasting "Blessed are you poor" to "Woe to you that are rich" (Luke 6:24). Matthew, who has a catechetical intention, takes a concern to make explicit the religious meaning of the word *poor* in Jewish spirituality and in Jesus' thinking by adding "in spirit." As for modern interpreters, some, like Matthew, emphasize the religious aspect of the word, while others, like Luke, emphasize the social aspect.

According to the group that emphasizes the religious aspect, "poor in spirit" points to an interior attitude more than to a social status. Jesus, they say, did not intend to call a particular social class blessed. Only a spiritual disposition can be connected to a spiritual reality like the kingdom. It is true that real poverty can be an advantageous path to poverty of spirit, and Jesus repeats that in countless ways. However, one should not think that this beatitude is dealing with the working class or the so-called "people of the land"[1] in Judaism of that time. The true gospel poor are those who depend on God and have staked everything on him in faith. In Judaism of that time, the word *poor* was practically synonymous with *holy* (*hasid*) and *pious*.[2] The Fathers of the church made "poor in spirit" almost a synonym for *humble*.[3]

Those who favor the text from Luke emphasize the social significance of this beatitude, understanding by the word *poor* primarily a social condition, an actual status. According to them, the traditional interpretation places too much emphasis on the interior disposition of the poor and too little on the nature of the kingdom that is to come. The beatitudes, they say, are above all a revelation of the mercy and justice that characterize the kingdom of God. They contain more of a revelation about God than about human beings and the poor.

The word used in the Gospel to indicate the poor (*ptochoi*) means the indigent, the unfortunate, the hungry—those who are in need of the basic necessities of life. The corresponding Hebrew word, *anawim*, originally meant the people who were "bowed down," that is, crushed, humiliated, oppressed.

Why, we can ask, should those people be favored by God? It

is not because of their particular religious merits, one could answer, or because of their good disposition but because God, insofar as he is a just king, must defend the defenseless. The poor, according to Old Testament thinking, are those who are protected by the king.

But how does one explain, in that case, the persistence of poverty and the oppression of the poor both in Israel and also around Jesus, through whom the kingdom of God has already come? These contradictory facts do not point us to abandoning our conviction about God's royal justice but rather to projecting that justice into the future, into the kingdom of God at the end of time. Then the poor will be vindicated from all those who oppress them; then they will truly enjoy the benefits of God's loving care.[4]

The Theological Explanation Is Insufficient

In these two main interpretations of the beatitude about the poor, one, as we saw, puts more emphasis on poverty as an attitude of the soul, and the other more emphasis on poverty as a social condition. In both cases redemption from poverty comes from the kingdom of God, but in the first case it depends on a disposition in human beings, while in the second it depends only on an essential quality in God. Taken separately, neither of these two interpretations is fully satisfactory. The first is insufficient because it tends to exclude any social response to the reality of poverty. The second is insufficient because it excludes too drastically the interior disposition of the poor.

I would like to highlight in particular the drawbacks of the second interpretation, which turns poverty into a theological problem by making everything depend on God. It does not explain the close tie that exists in the Gospel between the concepts of poverty and humility, the tie between the favoring of the poor and the favoring of children. Moreover, this interpretation, narrowly understood, leads to no practical results. The great redemption of the poor, sociologically, should be accomplished by the kingdom of God. But then analyzing the nature of that kingdom, one can see that it brings no actual change for the poor, since it makes them neither richer nor more satisfied on the material level.

This second interpretation, however, is only seemingly more attentive to social concerns. It in fact presents the risk of exploiting poverty by making it merely an occasion in which God can demonstrate his sovereign justice. It also does not take into account that its fulfillment, in this case as well, would occur on a level quite different from that of promise and expectation: The poor are promised redemption from material poverty, but in the end it turns out to be a redemption only of a spiritual nature.

Jesus certainly is concerned with the real poor, but that is not what he has in mind when he proclaims the poor "blessed." What he has in mind concerning the real poor is shown when he states that what is done—or not done—to them is done to him and when he threatens hell, as in the parable of the rich glutton, to those who do not demonstrate concern for the poor (see Luke 16:19–31).

The difficulty for us arises from thinking of the categories of merit and virtue when the category of faith should be used instead. God is not induced to act on behalf of the poor because of their merits or their moral dispositions but because of their greater readiness to believe. God does not value what the poor have but what they do not have: self-sufficiency, a closed attitude, a presumption of being able to save themselves. To think otherwise would be like saying that the kingdom is offered first to publicans and prostitutes because God favors their current states rather than because those people are capable of reformation, while the self-righteous are not.

It is not a question of God's action depending on something that *comes before* it, because it clearly does not. What matters is knowing if God's action requires something *in response*. The poor must recognize and accept this preferential offer from God. In short, they should believe. "God," says Saint James, has "chosen those who are poor in the world to be rich in *faith*" (James 2:5, emphasis added).

The gospel beatitude "Blessed are the poor in spirit, for theirs is the kingdom of heaven" is read in the light of the pairing of grace and faith: "By grace you have been saved through faith" (Ephesians 2:8). In this beatitude the kingdom represents the offer of grace, and poverty of spirit represents the response of faith. The poor in spirit are the believing poor. It is as if Jesus were saying, "Blessed are you poor because you have believed," or, "Blessed are you if you believe." (We should not forget that he is addressing actual people who are following him, just as in the "woes" he is addressing those who have in fact rejected him.) Faith is the framework for each of Jesus' discourses.

The solution to the difficulty of the two Gospel perspectives is thus to be sought in their synthesis. We need to unite, not oppose, Luke's "poor" and Matthew's "poor in spirit." In adding "in spirit" to "poor," Matthew is performing not only a catechetical but also an interpretive exercise, and he is thereby highlighting an implicit but real aspect of the concept of the poor according to what Jesus had in mind.

Poverty in Christ's Life

The best exegesis of the beatitude about the poor is the life of Christ itself. Saint Paul writes, "Jesus Christ,... though he was rich, yet for your sake he became poor, so that by his poverty you might become rich" (2 Corinthians 8:9). There is no doubt that he is speaking here of the material poverty of Christ. He means that Christ, being rich (or having the standing of being rich), makes himself poor *materially* to enrich us *spiritually*. "He [took on] bodily poverty, in order to enrich us spiritually," comments Saint Thomas Aquinas.[5] He did not come to make people richer in terms of earthly goods but to make them sons and daughters of God and heirs of eternal life.

The poverty of Christ above all has a concrete, existential aspect that accompanies him from birth to death. Blessed Angela of Foligno has a rather profound passage on the poverty of the Savior:

This poverty was of three kinds.... Christ...exemplified the first degree of the most perfect poverty by choosing to live poorly and be poor, bereft of all earthly possession. He kept nothing for himself: no house, land, vineyard, coins, money.... He...[accepted] scarcity, hunger, thirst, cold, hard labor, austerity and hardship. Neither would he accept anything elegant or refined.... The second degree of poverty...was that he wanted to be poor with regard to relatives, friends.... The third and supreme degree of poverty was that Christ stripped himself of his very self, became poor with regard to his own power, wisdom, and glory.[6]

Blessed Angela refers to a poverty of things, a poverty of support and a poverty of prestige. This third kind of poverty is the most profound of all because it touches the sphere of being and not just the sphere of possessions. For Christ it consists in the very fact of his becoming man, of stripping himself, if not of his divine nature at least of all that his divine nature could have claimed for him in terms of glory, wealth and splendor. Saint Gregory of Nyssa exclaims, "What greater poverty is there for God than the form of a servant? What [is] more humble for the King of creation than to share in our poor nature?"[7] Poverty shines through Christ in its most sublime form not in his being poor (which can be an imposed or hereditary fact) but in *making himself* poor—out of love—to make others rich.

Nevertheless, there are perhaps some clichés about the material poverty of Jesus that need to be adjusted through a more attentive examination of the Gospels. As far as we know, Jesus did not belong, in terms of his social status, to the servant class, the lowest class of society at that time. He was a craftsman, and he earned his living with his own hands, which was clearly better than being a hired laborer. In his public life as well, the prestige of *rabbi* that he enjoyed, the invitations he received from well-to-do people, the friendships he enjoyed, like with Lazarus and his two sisters, the assistance he received from certain women of means (see Luke 8:2–3)—these are all things that prevent us from considering him as the poorest of the poor. The very statement "Foxes have holes, and birds of the air have nests; but the Son of man has nowhere to lay his head" (Luke 9:58) can be better explained in the context of his role as an itinerant preacher with no established home than by his not having a literal roof over his head, even if that could also be included.

From the strictly materialistic point of view, there certainly were people in his time who were much poorer than he, whole groups of dispossessed people on whom he had compassion on seeing them "harassed and helpless" (Matthew 9:36). In addition, among his future disciples, like certain ascetics and hermits of the desert, there were some who would surpass the Master in terms of austerity and purely material poverty.

The misunderstandings above stem from ascribing an excessive value to external and material manifestations of poverty. Jesus never claimed a preeminence for poverty the way he claimed a preeminence for charity, in saying that no one has greater love than to lay down his life for his friends (see John 15:13). He was also free about his poverty, just as he was free in eating and drinking to the point of being considered a drunkard and a glutton without being too concerned about that judgment. In terms of *ascesis* (self-discipline), the precursor, John the Baptist, was much more rigorous than he.

Jesus did not fall into the trap that some of his imitators later fell into of making material poverty absolute, measuring their degree of perfection on that basis and thereby ending up becoming rich in the worst possible thing there is: themselves and their own righteousness. There is no absolute measurement assigned to material things, no point beyond which a person cannot go. No matter how poor a person wants to be, he or she will discover that there is always someone poorer. There is no limit to material poverty.

What gives religious value to poverty is the motivation for which it is chosen, and in the case of Christ the motivation is love: "He was rich, yet for *your sake* he became poor, so that by his poverty you might become rich" (2 Corinthians 8:9, emphasis added). A gift is precious particularly when it is the result of self-denial, when one deprives oneself of what is given. And the Word, in a particular way, deprived himself of his divine riches to be able to become one of us. The poverty of God is an expression of his *agape*, of his being "love." The Cynic philosophers of Jesus' time lived in material poverty in certain respects more radical than his, but they were not inspired by love for human beings; rather they took on poverty as a challenge to demonstrate the independence and superiority of human beings over nature and over things.

To Be for the Poor and to Be Poor

With the coming of Christ we see a qualitative leap on the subject of poverty. It can be summarized this way: The Old Testament presents a God who is for the poor, while the New Testament presents a God who makes himself poor. The Old Testament is full of texts about a God who hears the cry of the poor, who has mercy on the weak and the poor, who defends the cause of the poor, who gives justice to the oppressed. Only the Gospel speaks to us about the God who becomes one of them, who chooses poverty and weakness for himself. Material poverty, formerly an evil to avoid, now becomes a good to cultivate, an ideal to pursue. This is the enormous innovation that Christ brings to it.

Thus the two essential components of gospel poverty are now clear: to be for the poor and to be poor. The history of Christian poverty is the history of the different approaches to these two requirements. It is reflected, for example, in the two different ways of interpreting the episode of the rich young man (see Matthew 19:16–22). At times what is emphasized is to "sell all" and at other times to "give to the poor," that is, at times stripping oneself of everything to follow Christ radically and at other times having a concern for the poor.[8]

In antiquity the interpretation of the Encratites—a radical movement that proposed total abstention (*engrateia*) from marriage and possessions—can be contrasted to the conciliatory interpretation by Clement of Alexandria. He risks, in turn, going to the opposite extreme when he affirms that what counts is not so much poverty but the use that one makes of riches: "He who holds possessions, and gold, and silver, and houses, as the gifts of God; and ministers from them to the God who gives them for the salvation of men... [t]his is he who is blessed by the Lord, and called poor in spirit."[9]

An initial synthesis and balance between the two positions is reached in the thinking of people like Saint Basil and Saint Augustine and in the monastic experience of their followers. Here the most rigorous personal poverty is combined with an equal concern for the poor and the sick. This becomes concrete in specific institutions that will serve, in some cases, as models for the future works of charity by the church.

In medieval times we see the repetition of this cycle in a new historical context. The church, and in particular the ancient monastic orders that became quite wealthy in the West, cultivates poverty at this time almost wholly in the form of assistance to the poor and to pilgrims, that is, in managing charitable institutions. On the other hand, from the beginning of the second millennium, there is the emergence of the so-called *pauper Christi* movements, which put the concrete exercise of poverty first and represent a return of the church to the simplicity and poverty of the gospel. The balance and the synthesis occur this time through the mendicant orders, which try to practice a radical divesting of everything along- side a loving care for the poor, the lepers and the slaves, and which try above all to live their poverty in communion with the church rather than in opposition to it.

With some needed qualifications we can perhaps catch sight of an analogous dialectic in our day. The explosion of social consciousness in the last two centuries about the prob- lem of the working class has again disrupted the balance; it has marginalized the ideal of voluntary poverty, chosen and lived for the sake of following Christ, in order to focus on the problem of the poor. A concern for the poor prevails over the ideal of a poor church. This is translated into countless new initiatives and institutions, especially in the spheres of edu- cation of poor children and of assistance to those who are the most neglected. The social doctrine of the church is a prod- uct of this spiritual climate as well.

It was the Second Vatican Council (especially because of the notable contribution of Cardinal Giacomo Lercaro) that brought the issue of "the church and poverty" back to the forefront. In the Dogmatic Constitution on the Church, we read in this regard:

Just as Christ carried out the work of redemption in poverty and oppression, so the Church is called to follow the same path.... Christ was sent by the Father "to bring good news to the poor[,]...to heal the contrite of heart" (Lk 4:18), "to seek and to save what was lost" (Lk 19:10).

Similarly, the Church encompasses with her love all those who are afflicted by human misery and she recognizes in those who are poor and who suffer, the image of her poor and suffering founder. She does all in her power to relieve their need and in them she strives to serve Christ.[10]

This text combines both aspects: being poor and being in service to the poor. This is not to say that these two aspects can and should be cultivated in equal measure by every believer or by every group of believers. We need, in fact, to take into account the doctrine of charisms and the different functions assigned to each member of the body of Christ. Saint Paul seems to include the voluntary renunciation of one's own goods for the sake of other people in the list of charisms. For Paul, in fact, giving in simplicity and giving all one has to the poor are charisms, just as in the same context prophecy, speaking in tongues and knowledge are charisms (see Romans 12:6–8; 1 Corinthians 13:3).

Through some of its members and religious orders, then, the church will proclaim the poor Christ to a greater degree and through others the Christ who takes upon himself the infirmities and diseases of the poor (see Matthew 8:17). The fullness of the Spirit and of the gifts is found in the church and not in any one believer. In the communion of the church, however, this fullness becomes the possession of all. If I love unity and remain committed to it, whatever someone has or does is mine. I belong in fact to that body that is poor and that takes concern for the poor. "Take away envy," Saint Augustine said, "and what I have is yours too."[11]

Consequently, we must banish animosity and judgment, substituting instead a reciprocal esteem for, and joy in, the good that God accomplishes through others. Those who work for social justice and the advancement of the poor (who often need many resources and structures) rejoice that there are others who live and proclaim the gospel in poverty and simplicity, and vice versa. The apostle exhorted, in a situation similar to this one, "Let us no more pass judgment on one another.... Let us then pursue what makes for peace and for mutual upbuilding" (Romans 14:13, 19).

Why Voluntary Poverty?

We still need to answer perhaps the most important question: Why did Christ introduce the ideal of voluntary poverty into the world? Why voluntarily renounce the things that God has created for human beings to enjoy? Is redemption possibly set in opposition to creation?

The answer lies in the reason behind Christ's proposition. It is clearly expressed in the text: the kingdom of heaven or the kingdom of God. Everything takes its meaning from the nature of this kingdom that is *already* present in the world but *not yet* fully and definitively established.

Because the kingdom of God is already present in the earth in the person and preaching of Jesus, we must not miss out on it but seize it, putting aside everything that could be an obstacle to it, including, if need be, even a hand or an eye (see Matthew 18:8–9). It is possible, in other words, to begin to live here and now the way we will live in the definitive establishment of the kingdom, where earthly goods no longer will have any value but where God will be all in all.

This is the rationale for a poverty that we can call *eschatological*, or *prophetic*, insofar as it announces the new heavens and the new earth. Poverty is prophetic because, with the example of detachment from earthly goods, it proclaims silently but effectively that there exists another good; it reminds us that the form of this world is passing away and that we do not have our permanent dwelling here because our homeland is in heaven.

The eschatological rationale—based on the sudden breaking in of the kingdom or, after Easter, on the expectation of the imminent return of Christ—continues to function in an ongoing though somewhat different way. Christians do not have a permanent citizenship here; they belong to another city. Because of this we should not rely too much on the goods of the present time, since they will need to be left behind suddenly. The eschatological rationale continues to function, then, in the form of a hope for eternal goods.

Thus we speak of the first characteristic of the kingdom as something that has in essence already come. However, in another sense the kingdom still needs to come and is on its way to filling the whole earth. Therefore, there is a need for some people who will dedicate themselves entirely to its coming, free of every earthly tie or compromise that could hinder such a proclamation. If the gospel is to reach "to the end of the earth" (Acts 1:8), it is necessary that its messengers, like racers in a stadium, be light, free and unencumbered, so that "the word of the Lord may speed on" (2 Thessalonians 3:1).

This is the *missionary* or *apostolic* reason for poverty, highlighted especially in the dispatching discourses of Jesus: "Take nothing for your journey, no staff, nor bag, nor bread, nor money; and do not have two tunics" (Luke 9:3).

The Contemporary Relevance of the Beatitude on Poverty
The beatitude about the poor is of great relevance in the historical context in which we live, which is marked by a concern for ecology and the preservation of creation. One way of living the gospel beatitude that is possible and accessible to everyone is to return to a moderate and temperate use of things, to a simple lifestyle that allows us to enjoy the goods of creation without abusing or wasting them.

We need this invitation, especially in the wealthy nations of the Northern Hemisphere. We are tempted to replace things endlessly: clothes, cars, computers and other electronic devices. "Use it and pitch it" summarizes our civilization. At times this takes on extreme forms.

Francis of Assisi used to say to his brothers, "I have never been a thief concerning alms, in getting them or using them beyond necessity. Always have I taken less than I needed, lest I should defraud other poor folk of their portion, for to do the contrary would have been theft."[12] We should be able to say the same thing about the goods in creation: "I have not stolen resources that were destined for future generations: water, energy, lumber for paper-making and so on." Whatever we use in excess, directly or indirectly, we are taking away from others who now live on the earth or who will come after us.

I would like to share the words of an English writer, Jerome K. Jerome, a humorist who in this case, however, is speaking seriously. The experience of a boat trip on the Thames, going against the current, suggested to him this observation on life:

How many people, on that voyage [of life], load up the boat till it is ever in danger of swamping with a store of foolish things which they think essential to the pleasure and comfort of the trip, but which are really only useless lumber.... Let your boat of life be light, packed only with what you need—a homely home and simple pleasures, one or two friends, worth the name, someone to love and someone to love you, a cat, a dog, and a pipe or two, enough to eat and enough to wear, and a little more than enough to drink.... You will find the boat easier to pull then, and it will not be so liable to upset.... You will have time to think as well as to work. Time to drink in life's sunshine.[13]

This is not exactly the gospel ideal of poverty in the kingdom, but at least it shows that the ideal of simplicity is not contrary to human happiness and is instead a powerful ally.

Another attitude that the gospel beatitude about poverty encourages is contemplation. We need to discover and esteem the special mode of possession that contemplation brings. It is a way of possessing things in a more profound manner—with one's soul and not only with the senses and the body.

Saint Paul defines apostles, and indirectly all Christians, "as having nothing, and yet possessing everything" (2 Corinthians 6:10). Contemplation brings about this miracle: It allows us to own things without hoarding them for ourselves and without depriving others of them. When someone has ownership rights to something—a park, a forest, a seaside beach, a small lake—it belongs only to that person, and everyone else is excluded. In contemplation a thousand people can enjoy that same lake and park without taking away anyone else's enjoyment.

Chapter Two

BLESSED ARE YOU THAT WEEP NOW, FOR YOU SHALL LAUGH

The beatitudes are not an outdated legal code that the church has to accept and transmit as faithfully as possible. They are a source of perennial inspiration because the one who proclaimed them is risen and alive. What the French poet Charles Péguy says about all of Christ's words applies to the beatitudes as well:

> Jesus [did not] give us dead words
> That we are to shut up in little boxes
> ...
> And that we are to preserve in rancid oil.
> ...
> But he gave us living words
> To nourish [us].
> ...
> Words of life, living words can only be preserved alive.
> ... [We] [a]re summoned to nourish the word of the son of God.
> ... [I]t is our duty,
> It is our task, it is our responsibility

To see that it is heard world without end,

To make it resound.[1]

A New Relationship Between Pleasure and Pain

Let us reflect on the second beatitude, "Blessed are those who mourn, for they shall be comforted" (Matthew 5:4). In some manuscripts and modern translations, the order of the second and third beatitudes—those who mourn and the meek—is reversed, but this has no bearing on their significance.

In the Gospel of Luke there are four beatitudes in the form of a direct discourse that are reinforced by a contrary "woe." The same beatitude in Luke is phrased this way: "Blessed are you that weep now, for you shall laugh.... Woe to you that laugh now, for you shall mourn and weep" (Luke 6:21, 25).

Notice first of all that this is the only beatitude that is based on the idea of *contrapasso*, a kind of retributive justice. In the other beatitudes the connection between the present and the future situation is based on fulfillment: The poor are blessed because the kingdom of heaven is theirs; the meek shall inherit the earth. Here instead there is a reversal between the beatitude and its reward, a shift from one emotional state to its opposite: from weeping to laughter or, vice versa, from laughter to weeping.

The most extraordinary message is enclosed precisely in the structure of the Lucan version of this beatitude. It enables us to understand the revolution that the gospel has brought concerning the problem of pleasure and pain. The point of departure—common to religious and secular thinking—is the observation that pleasure and pain are inseparable in this life. They follow after one another with the same regularity that waves in the sea crest and recede behind a swimmer.

Human beings try desperately to detach these conjoined twins, to isolate pleasure from pain. But in vain. The very same disordered pleasure turns back and transforms itself into suffering. And this can happen spontaneously and tragically or a little at a time, insofar as the nature of pleasure is transitory and soon produces weariness and boredom. It is a lesson that comes to us daily in the news and that human beings have expressed in a thousand ways in art and literature. In the words of the pagan poet Lucretius, "In the very fountain of delights, there rises / Something of bitterness that chokes even among the roses."[2]

Illicit pleasure is deceptive because it promises what it cannot give. Before being tasted it seems to offer you infinity and eternity. But once it is used up, you find yourself empty-handed. It is the tragic message of so much modern poetry. The "flowers of evil" have barely been picked, Charles Baudelaire tells us, when they begin to wilt already and give off a rotting odor.[3]

The Bible says it has an answer, an explanation, for this drama of human existence. From the very beginning there has been choice for human beings, made possible by their freedom and by their nature consisting of spirit and matter. That choice has led them to direct the irrepressible desire for joy exclusively toward visible things—although it was given to them so that they might aspire to the enjoyment of the infinite Good, who is God.

When a pleasure is against the law of God, symbolized by Adam and Eve in their eating the forbidden fruit, God permits pain and death to follow it, more as a remedy than as a punishment. He does so lest, hurriedly acting on their selfishness and their basic instincts, human beings destroy themselves as well as their neighbors. Therefore we see pain adhering to pleasure, like its shadow.

Christ has finally broken this chain: "For the joy that was set before him [Jesus] endured the cross" (Hebrews 12:2). He does, in short, the opposite of what Adam, and every human being, does. Saint Maximus the Confessor writes, "For, unlike that of everyone else, the Lord's death was not the payment of a death incurred because of pleasure, but was on the contrary a challenge thrown down to pleasure; and so through this death He utterly destroys that justly deserved death which ends human life."[4]

Rising from the dead, Christ inaugurated a new type of pleasure that does not *precede* pain as its cause but *follows* it as its fruit. And this is the case not only for purely spiritual pleasure but also for every genuine pleasure, including the one that man and woman experience in the reciprocal gift of each other in generating life and in seeing their children and grandchildren grow; it includes the pleasure of art and creativity, of beauty, of friendship, of a task well done; it includes every joy that comes from a duty fulfilled.

All of this is wonderfully proclaimed in this beatitude that contrasts the sequence of *laughter-weeping* to the sequence of *weeping-laughter*. It is not a question of a simple reversal of order. The difference, an infinite one, is the fact that in the order proposed by Jesus, it is pleasure, not pain, that will have the last word and—what matters even more—that this last word will continue for eternity.

Christ's judgment on laughter and weeping does not make sense only in the eternal scheme of things, however. It also sheds light on this present life, at least in part. It is a question of understanding what that initial word "blessed" means and of knowing which blessedness or happiness is in play. It does not involve a happiness only for the senses, a simple euphoria and lightheartedness, but it involves a complete and ongoing well-being for the whole person. Tears and affliction are proclaimed blessed because they make people more mature, more profound, more authentic, more sympathetic to the suffering of others. In a word, they make people more human.

The gospel does not condemn happiness and joy at all. The words *joy* and *celebration* recur, one could say, on every page. Laughter and celebration only become signs of selfishness when, instead of signaling a time of relaxation and a time away from hard work, they become an idol, something that claims to be a right and a permanent condition of life even at the expense of others' suffering.

The case of laughter and happiness that comes through clowns and comedians is a different matter. Their goal is to make people laugh, to entertain and instruct others, to communicate a joyful time to everyone. It is a gift for every-one, at least insofar as it keeps itself on the level of art and does not descend into vulgarity and spiteful satire, that is, when it makes people laugh without ridiculing others.

The film *Life Is Beautiful* by Roberto Benigni, for example, was so well liked because the comic element is placed in the service of love—in this case, the love of a father who, through joy and laughter, wants to spare his son the horrors of depor-tation and of a concentration camp. The protagonist is suf-fering, but he makes the effort to communicate joy, and whether the director intended it or not, this falls within the framework of the gospel beatitude in its own way. Christ's beatitude is not meant to be understood only in the future—"Blessed are those who mourn now because someday they will be comforted"—but in the present as well: "Blessed are those who accept being afflicted so that others around them can be comforted."

Where Is Your God?

We need to understand exactly who the people are that Christ proclaimed blessed in their mourning and weeping. Today's exegetes almost unanimously reject that they are the people afflicted only in an objective or sociological sense, that is, people that Jesus would proclaim blessed simply because they suffer and weep. The subjective element—the reason for their weeping—is the determining factor here.

And what is that reason? The Fathers and ancient spiritual authors insisted on a *penitential* reason, tears of repentance for sins. Modern authors propose instead an *existential* reason: the weeping of people who feel that they are strangers on earth and are far from their homeland, of people who grieve for the terrible suffering that is in the world.[5] This is a cosmic weeping, so to speak, in line with the Pauline groaning of creation and of human beings awaiting their full redemption (see Romans 8:19–23) or with the Virgilian *sunt lacrimae rerum:* "They weep here / For how the world goes."[6]

I believe that we should not restrict the field to just those two reasons. The surest way to discover the kind of weeping and mourning that are proclaimed blessed by Christ is to see why people in the Bible weep and why he himself weeps in the Gospel. We discover that there is a weeping of repentance like Peter's after his betrayal; there is a weeping "with those who weep" (Romans 12:15), that is, of compassion for the sorrow of others, as Jesus weeps with the widow of Nain and with the sisters of Lazarus; there is the weeping of exiles who long for their homeland, like that of the Israelites on the riverbanks of Babylon; and many other kinds.

I would like to highlight two of the reasons for which people in the Bible and Jesus weep that seem particularly appropriate to meditate on at this present time. In Psalm 42 we read:

My tears have been my food,
   day and night,
while men say to me continually,
   "Where is your God?"

. . .

As with a deadly wound in my body,

   my adversaries taunt me,

while they say to me continually,

   "Where is your God?" (Psalm 42:3, 10)

The sadness of this believer over the arrogant rejection of God all around him has never had more basis than it does today. After a period of relative silence following the end of Marxist atheism, we are witnessing the fiery return of a militant and aggressive atheism of a scientific or pseudo-scientific character. The titles of some recent books tell the story: *Atheist Manifesto*,[7] *The God Delusion*,[8] *The End of Faith*,[9] *Creation without God*,[10] *An Ethic without God*,[11] *God Is Not Great: How Religion Poisons Everything*.[12]

In one of these kinds of books, the Italian author asserts that since societies have developed a variety of standard methods for establishing or verifying something, whoever affirms the existence of a being that is not knowable through these methods must shoulder the burden of proof. It seems legitimate to him that until there is proof to the contrary, God does not exist.[13]

We could, with these same kinds of arguments, demonstrate that love does not exist either, since it is not verifiable through scientific methods. The fact is that proof for the existence of God is not found in biology books or laboratories but in life—in the life of Christ first of all, then of the saints and of the innumerable witnesses to faith. It is also found in the signs and wonders, which are so often disregarded, that Jesus himself did to confirm his truth.

It is true, as Gotthold Lessing observes, that miracles serve as proof to those who witness them and not necessarily to those who only hear about them,[14] but miracles are happening today right in front of our eyes. People should not reject *a priori* their possibility without making the effort to examine them, and they should not deny all miracles outright only because it can be demonstrated that some of them are not genuine.

The reason for a believer's sadness, as for the psalmist, is the helplessness that is felt when faced by the challenge, "Where is your God?" With his mysterious silence God calls the believer to share his weakness and failure, promising victory only under those conditions: "The weakness of God is stronger than men" (1 Corinthians 1:25).

To be sincere and fruitful, the tears of the believer must be poured out not only because of unbelievers but for the sake of unbelievers, through genuine compassion. It does not matter if those tears are rejected or ridiculed. The philosopher Søren Kierkegaard writes:

There is so much talk about human distress and wretchedness —I try to understand it and have also had some intimate acquaintance with it—there is so much talk about wasting a life, but only that person's life was wasted who went on living so deceived by life's joys or its sorrows that he never became decisively and eternally conscious as spirit, as self, or, what amounts to the same thing, never became aware and in the deepest sense never gained the impression that there is a God and that "he," he himself, his self, exists before this God.... I think that I could weep an eternity over the existence of such wretchedness![15]

Mother Teresa of Calcutta, who encountered a great deal of poverty and misery, used to say that the most terrible poverty is that of people who think they can do without God.

"Let the Priests, the Ministers of the Lord, Weep"

There is another kind of weeping in the Bible that we should reflect on; It is not a weeping for others but for ourselves. The prophets speak about it. Ezekiel relates a vision he had one day. The powerful voice of God cries out to a mysterious person "clothed in linen, with a writing case at his side.... 'Go through the city, through Jerusalem, and put a mark upon the foreheads of the men who sigh and groan over all the abominations that are committed in it'" (Ezekiel 9:2, 4).

The church has "sighed and groaned" in recent times for the abominations committed inside of it by some of its own ministers and pastors. It has paid a very high price for cases of pedophilia by the clergy. It has taken measures and made strict rules to prevent the abuses from being repeated. The moment has come to do something else as well: to weep before God, to grieve as God grieves for the offense done to the body of Christ and the scandal committed against "the least of his brothers." This is the right attitude, so that good can truly come from all this evil, and a reconciliation between the people and God and their own priests can occur.

> Blow the trumpet in Zion;
>> sanctify a fast;
> call a solemn assembly;
>
> ...
>
> Between the vestibule and the altar
>> let the priests, the ministers of the LORD, weep
> and say, "Spare your people, O LORD,
>> and make not your heritage a reproach,
>> a byword among the nations.
> Why should they say among the peoples,
>> 'Where is their God ?'" (Joel 2:15, 17)

These words from the prophet Joel extend a call to us. Can we not do the same thing today, that is, call for a day of fasting and repentance, at least at the local and national levels where the problem was the worst, to publicly express repentance before God and solidarity with the victims?

I have the courage to say this because of what Benedict XVI said to the bishops from a Catholic country during a recent *ad limina* visit: "The wounds caused by such acts run deep, and it is an urgent task to rebuild confidence and trust where these have been damaged.... In this way the Church...will grow stronger and be ever more capable of giving witness to the redemptive power of the Cross of Christ."[16]

But we should, in addition, not leave the unfortunate brothers who were the cause of the harm without a word of hope. Concerning the case of incest in the community at Corinth, the apostle ruled, "You are to deliver this man to Satan for the destruction of the flesh, that his spirit may be saved in the day of the Lord Jesus" (1 Corinthians 5:5). The salvation of the sinner, even more than his punishment, was the concern of the apostle's heart.

These brothers of ours have been stripped of everything: ministry, honor, freedom. No one knows for sure the actual degree of moral responsibility in each individual case. They are at the bottom of the heap; they have become outcasts. If in this condition they are touched by grace, if they mourn for the evil they have caused, then they unite their weeping to that of the church, and the beatitude of those who mourn and weep becomes a beatitude for them. They can be close to Christ, who is a friend to outcasts, more so than to many others, myself included, who are full of their own respectability and are perhaps led, like the Pharisees, to judge those who make mistakes.

This does not release us, of course, from doing what we can to collaborate on every level with human justice so that these scandals are not repeated and to seek to help the victims of abuse, providing spiritual help as well.

The Best Tears
Up to this point we have considered some reasons for Christians today to mourn and weep, but I cannot end without noting that there is another kind of tears. One can weep from sorrow but also from deep emotion and joy. The most

beautiful tears are those that fill our eyes when, enlightened by the Holy Spirit, we "taste and see that the LORD is good!" (Psalm 34:8).

When one is in this state of grace, he or she marvels that the world and we ourselves do not fall on our knees and weep with deep emotion and amazement. Tears like these must have fallen from Augustine's eyes when he wrote in his *Confessions*, "How have you loved us, O good Father, who did not spare your only Son, but delivered him up for us sinners. How have you loved us."[17] Tears like these were shed by Blaise Pascal the night he had the revelation of the God of Abraham, Isaac and Jacob, who reveals himself in the Gospel; on a slip of paper (found sewn into his jacket after his death), he had written, "Joy, joy, joy, tears of joy!"[18] I believe that the tears with which the sinful woman bathed the feet of Jesus were not only tears of repentance but also tears of gratitude and joy.

If one can weep in heaven, then this is the kind of weeping that heaven would have. Saint Symeon the New Theologian, the saint of tears, lived around the year 1000 in Istanbul, the former Constantinople. He is the most striking example in the history of Christian spirituality of tears of repentance that become transformed into tears of wonder and silence. He records in one of his works, "I wept and lived in an unutterable joy."[19] Paraphrasing the beatitude of those who mourn, he says, "Blessed are they who ever weep bitterly for their sins, for the light shall seize them and change the bitter into sweet."[20]

One day in the midst of his tears, Saint Symeon experienced such a strong joy that he exclaimed, "What can be greater than this? It is enough for me to be in this state even after death!" The voice of Christ answered, "You are indeed too faint-hearted to be contented with this. Compared with the blessing to come, this is like a description of heaven on paper."[21]

Chapter Three

BLESSED ARE THE MEEK, FOR THEY SHALL INHERIT THE EARTH

To discover who the meek are whom Jesus proclaims blessed, it would be good to review briefly the various words used for "the meek" (*praeis*) in modern translations. Italian has two words: *miti* ("the meek") and *mansueti* ("the mild"). This second word is the word used in the Spanish translation, *los mansos*. In French the word is translated as *doux*, literally meaning "sweet," those who have the virtue of sweetness.[1] In German different translations alternate. Luther translated the word as "the meek, the sweet" (*Sanftmütigen*). In the *Einheits Bibel*, the ecumenical German translation of the Bible, the meek are those who "do no violence," the nonviolent. Along this line, some emphasize the objective and sociological dimension of the word and translate the Greek word as "the weak," "the powerless" (*Machtlosen*). Some English translations see a nuance of kindness and courtesy in the beatitude and translate *praeis* as "the gentle."

Each of these translations highlights a true but partial component of this word in the beatitude. We need to keep all of these meanings together, rather than isolate just one of them, if we want to have an idea of the original richness of this Gospel word. Two frequent associations in the Bible and in ancient Christian *parenesis* (moral instruction) can help us arrive at the full sense of *meekness*. One combines *meekness* and *humility*; the other combines *meekness* and *patience*. The first association highlights the interior disposition from which meekness flows, while the second emphasizes the attitude one should have in dealings with one's neighbor: forbearance, gentleness, respect, kindness. These are the same characteristics that the apostle highlights when he speaks of love (see 1 Corinthians 13:4–5).

Two Keys to Reading the Beatitudes

Jesus says, "Blessed are the meek" (Matthew 5:5), and in another passage from that same Gospel, he says, "Learn from me; for I am gentle [meek] and lowly in heart" (Matthew 11:29). We can infer from this that the beatitudes are not just a nice ethical program that the Master outlines theoretically, so to speak, for his followers. They are the self-portrait of Jesus! He is the one who is genuinely poor, meek, pure of heart and persecuted for righteousness. "We have found the genuine poor man," exclaims Saint Augustine, and he is "a member of the poor man who became poor for our sake."[2]

This point affords us an occasion to highlight the two different basic interpretations of the Gospel beatitudes that have occurred in the course of history: the moral interpretation and the Christological interpretation. A moral interpretation, for example, is given by Saint Thomas Aquinas, who deals with the beatitudes in the moral section of his *Summa* in the context of virtues and gifts.[3] According to the moral interpretation, in the beatitudes Jesus is outlining an ideal of perfection for his disciples that transcends the law. The requirements the beatitudes set forth can sometimes appear to be unattainable, and for that reason they are not given as precepts but only as beatitudes. In the scholastic distinction between gospel precepts and counsels, they fall into the category of counsels, the so-called "supererogatory" works (works that exceed the minimal requirements of morality).

Luther holds to this moral interpretation, but in a certain sense he reverses it. The unattainable demands of Jesus serve only to reveal to human beings their own sin and their powerlessness to do good, leading them therefore to put their trust only in the grace of Christ. The beatitudes have an "accusatory" value, so to speak, just as, according to Paul, all of the ancient Law does. They do not indicate what we *should do* but what we *cannot do* on our own.

For Saint Thomas as well, the beatitudes, like all moral precepts of the gospel, would be "the letter [that]...would kill, unless there were the inward presence of the healing grace of faith."[4] However, this does not mean he reduces their purpose to a pure and simple "revelation of sin."

The key to a Christological reading, on the other hand, is the one that interprets the beatitudes not as a mirror to human sin but as an affirmation about Christ and the "new man" modeled after him.[5] The focus here is on the positive, not the negative. This is what I meant earlier when I said that the beatitudes are fundamentally the self-portrait of Jesus.

As always, the thing to do is not to oppose these two ways of understanding the beatitudes but to keep them together. They certainly have a moral significance, and as such they require acceptance by and the cooperation of human beings, but their foundation is Christological: They tell us who Jesus is. Their moral significance inevitably arises precisely because of our obligation to imitate Christ. We can speak in both cases of a Christological reading of the beatitudes, provided that we correctly consider Christ as a gift to receive through faith and, at the same time, as a model to imitate through works.

This is where, I believe, we find the limitation in Mahatma Gandhi's approach to the Sermon on the Mount, which he admired so much. For him the sermon could be considered apart from the historical person of Christ. "I should not care," he once said, "if it was proved by someone that the man called Jesus never lived, and what was narrated in the *Gospels* was a figment of the writer's imagination. For, the *Sermon on the Mount* would still be true for me."[6]

It is, on the contrary, precisely the person and life of Christ that make the beatitudes and the whole Sermon on the Mount something more than a splendid utopian ethic. The life and person of Christ represent a fulfillment of the beatitudes in history from which everyone can draw strength, through the mystical communion that unites a person to the Savior. The beatitudes do not belong solely to the realm of obligation but also to the realm of grace.

Jesus, the Meek One

If the beatitudes are the self-portrait of Christ, the first thing to do in commenting on each of them is to see how he lived them. The Gospels, from beginning to end, demonstrate the meekness of Christ in both its aspects of humility and patience. It is Jesus, as we have seen, who proposes himself as the model for meekness. Matthew applies to him the words describing the Servant of God in Isaiah 42:2–3:

He will not wrangle or cry aloud,

. . .

he will not break a bruised reed
    or quench a smoldering wick. (Matthew 12:19–20)

His entry into Jerusalem, riding on a donkey, is seen as an example of the meek king who shuns any idea of violence and war (see Matthew 21:4–5).

The ultimate proof of Christ's meekness, though, is in his passion. There was no display of anger, no threat: "When he was reviled, he did not revile in return; when he suffered, he did not threaten" (1 Peter 2:23). This trait of Christ's personality was so stamped on the memory of his disciples that Saint Paul, wanting to persuade the Corinthians by invoking something precious and sacred, writes to them, "I... entreat you, by the meekness [*prautes*] and gentleness [*epieikeia*] of Christ" (2 Corinthians 10:1).

But Jesus did far more than give us an example of heroic meekness and patience. He made meekness and nonviolence the signs of true greatness. Greatness will no longer consist in lifting oneself up above others, above the crowd, but in the abasing of oneself to serve and lift others up. On the cross, Augustine says, Jesus reveals that true victory does not consist in making victims but in making oneself a victim: *Victor quia victima*, "Victor because victim."[7]

Nietzsche, as we know, opposed this vision, calling it a "slave morality" prompted by the natural "resentment" of the weak against the strong.[8] By preaching humility and meekness, making oneself small, turning the other cheek, Christianity introduced, according to him, a kind of cancer into humanity that has extinguished its energy and destroyed its vitality.

For some time now we have seen the attempt to absolve Nietzsche of every accusation, to domesticate and even to Christianize him. Some say that at the core he is not really against Christ but against the Christians who in a certain era preached self-denial for its own sake, disdaining life and disparaging the body. They hold that everyone, beginning with Hitler, has distorted the true thinking of this philosopher. They say that Nietzsche is actually a prophet of a new age, the precursor of the postmodern era.

There has been a single voice, we could say, opposing this tendency, the voice of the French thinker René Girard. According to him, all these attempts do an injustice above all to Nietzsche. With an insight that was truly unique for his time, Nietzsche understood the true crux of the problem: the irreducible alternative between paganism and Christianity. Paganism proposes the sacrifice of the weak in favor of the strong and of progress; Christianity exalts the sacrifice of the strong in favor of the weak. It is difficult not to see an objective nexus between Nietzsche's approach and Hitler's program to eliminate entire groups of people for the advancement of civilization and the purity of the race.

Christianity is not the only target of this philosopher; Christ is a target as well. "Dionysius versus the 'Crucified': there you have the antithesis," he exclaims in one of his posthumous fragments.[9]

The greatest boast of modern society—a concern for the victims, siding with the weak and oppressed, the defense of life that is threatened—is actually a direct product of the gospel revolution. However, through "a paradoxical competition of mimetic rivalries,"[10] this concern is now claimed by other movements to be their achievement, even in opposition to Christianity.[11]

It is not true that the gospel quells the desire to do great things and to excel. Jesus says, "*If any one would be first*, he must be last of all and servant of all" (Mark 9:35, emphasis added). It is therefore lawful, and even recommended, that a person should wish to be first, but it is the road to get there that has changed. It is not by lifting ourselves up over others, even crushing them if they are in the way, but by abasing ourselves to elevate others together with us.

Meekness and Tolerance

The beatitude about the meek has become extraordinarily relevant in the debate on religion and violence that intensified after September 11, 2001. It reminds us Christians, in particular, that the gospel leaves no room for doubt. The Gospels do not have exhortations to nonviolence mixed in with opposite kinds of exhortations. Christians in certain eras may have failed in this regard, but the gospel is clear, and the church can turn to it in every age to be inspired, certain of finding only truth and holiness there.

The Gospel says that "he who does not believe will be condemned" (Mark 16:16), but that means condemned in heaven, not on earth—by God, not by men. "When they persecute you in one town," Jesus says, "flee to the next" (Matthew 10:23). He does not say, "Attack that town with sword and fire."

On one occasion, two of Jesus' disciples, James and John, not having been well received in a certain Samaritan village, said to Jesus, "Lord, do you want us to bid fire come down from heaven and consume them?" Jesus, however, "turned and rebuked them" (Luke 9:54, 55). Many manuscripts also report the tone of his reproof: "You do not know what manner of spirit you are of; for the Son of man came not to destroy men's lives but to save them."[12]

The famous *compelle entrare*—"compel people to come in" (Luke 14:23)—with which Saint Augustine justifies, even though reluctantly,[13] his approval of the imperial laws against the Donatists[14] that will later serve to justify force against heretics, is due to an obvious forcing of the Gospel text, the result of a mechanical or literalistic reading of the Bible.

Jesus places that command in the mouth of a man who has prepared a great banquet, and when the guests refuse to come, he tells the servants to go into the highways and byways of the city and "bring in the poor and maimed and blind and lame" (see Luke 14:15–24). It is clear from this context that compelling them only means using friendly insistence. The poor and the maimed, like all unfortunate people, could feel embarrassed to present themselves at the palace, badly dressed as they are. "Overcome their resistance," recommends the master; "tell them to not be afraid to come." How often have we ourselves said in similar circumstances, "He pressed me hard to accept," knowing full well that the insistence was a sign of good will and not of violence?

A book about Jesus that has caused much comment recently in Italy attributes this sentence to him: "But as for these enemies of mine, who did not want me to reign over them, bring them here and slay them before me" (Luke 19:27). The authors conclude that "this is the kind of statement to which supporters of 'holy war' make reference."[15] It needs to be clarified that Luke does not attribute such words to Jesus but to the king in the parable, and we know that we cannot transfer the significance of all the details in a parable story to reality, and in any case, those details must be transferred from the material to the spiritual plane. The metaphorical meaning of these words is that accepting or rejecting Jesus is not without consequences. It is a question of life and death, but spiritual—not physical—life and death. Holy war is not at issue here.

With Meekness and Reverence

But let us move on from apologetic considerations to try to see how we can make the beatitude about the meek a light for our own Christian life. There is a pastoral application of this beatitude already evident in the First Letter of Peter. It deals with the Christian dialogue with the outside world: "In your hearts reverence Christ as Lord. Always be prepared to make a defense to any one who calls you to account for the hope that is in you, yet do it with gentleness [*prautes*, meekness] and reverence" (1 Peter 3:15).

From antiquity there have been two types of apologetics: one has Tertullian as its model and the other has Justin Martyr. The first aims to defeat the opponent, the other to convince. Tertullian (or one of his disciples) wrote a treatise called *Adversus Judeos* (*Against the Jews*); Justin wrote *The Dialogue With Trypho* (a Jew living in Greece). Both of these approaches have had a following in Christian literature (our own Giovanni Papini[16] was certainly closer to Tertullian than to Justin), but of course we prefer Justin's today. Benedict XVI's encyclical *God Is Love* is an illustrative example of a respectful and constructive presentation of Christian values that explains the Christian hope "with gentleness and reverence."

The martyr Saint Ignatius of Antioch proposed this attitude, which is always relevant, to Christians of his time in their dealings with the outside world: "When they are angry with you, be meek; answer their words of pride by your humility."[17]

The promise tied to the beatitude about the meek—"they shall inherit the earth"—is actualized on different levels, ending with the definitive Promised Land of eternal life, but certainly one of the levels is the human one. The "earth" represents the hearts of human beings. The meek win people's trust; they attract souls. The saint of meekness and mildness par excellence, Saint Francis de Sales, used to say, "One can catch more flies with a spoonful of honey than with a hundred barrels of vinegar."[18]

Learn From Me, for I Am Meek

We could spend a long time on these kinds of pastoral applications for the beatitude of the meek, but let us move on to a more personal application. Jesus says, "Learn from me; for I am gentle [meek]" (Matthew 11:29).

One could object that Jesus did not always show himself to be meek! He says, for example, not to oppose the wicked, and "if any one strikes you on the right cheek, turn to him the other also" (Matthew 5:39). However, when one of the guards strikes him on the cheek during his trial before the Sanhedrin, it is not recorded that he turned the other cheek but that he calmly responded, "If I have spoken wrongly, bear witness to the wrong; but if I have spoken rightly, why do you strike me?" (John 18:23).

This shows that not everything in the Sermon on the Mount is to be followed mechanically and literally. In line with his style and the requirements of oral teaching, Jesus uses hyperboles and highly imaginative language in order to impress a certain idea more strongly on the minds of his disciples. In the case of turning the other cheek, for example, the important part is not the gesture of turning the other cheek (which at times could even appear to be provocative) but of not responding to violence with violence, of overcoming anger with calmness. In this sense his answer to the guard is an example of divine meekness.

To measure the extent of this meekness, we only need to compare it to the reaction of his apostle Paul (who was a saint) in an analogous situation. When Paul is on trial before the Sanhedrin, and the high priest Ananias orders Paul to be struck on the mouth, he answers, "God shall strike you, you whitewashed wall!" (Acts 23:3).

Another ambiguity should be clarified. In the same Sermon on the Mount Jesus says, "Whoever insults his brother shall be liable to the council, and whoever says, 'You fool!' shall be liable to the hell of fire" (Matthew 5:22). But many times in the Gospel he addresses the scribes and Pharisees as "hypocrites" and "blind fools" (see Matthew 23:15, 17); he reproves his disciples, calling them "foolish men, and slow of heart to believe" (Luke 24:25).

Here again the explanation is simple. We need to distinguish between injuring others and correction. Jesus condemns words spoken in anger that are meant to offend someone, not the words that aim to help a person become aware of his or her error and to correct it. A father who says to his son, "You are undisciplined and disobedient," is not intending to insult him but to correct him. Moses is characterized by Scripture as "very meek, more than all men that were on the face of the earth" (Numbers 12:3), but yet we hear him exclaim to the people of Israel, "Do you thus repay the LORD, / you foolish and senseless people?" (Deuteronomy 32:6).

The deciding factor is whether the person is speaking out of love or out of hate. "Love and do what you will," Augustine used to say.[19] If you love, whether you correct or you let something go, it will be out of love. Love does no harm to one's neighbor. From the root of love, as from a good tree, only good fruit can come.

This brings us to the very terrain of the beatitude about the meek, the heart. Jesus says, "Learn from me; for I am gentle [meek] and lowly *in heart*" (Matthew 11:29, emphasis added). This is where true meekness is determined. It is out of the heart, he says, that murders, wickedness and slander come (see Mark 7:21–22), just as lava, ash and fiery rocks come out of the internal boiling of a volcano. The greatest explosions of violence, war and quarrels begin secretly from "your passions that are at war in your members" (James 4:1–2). Just as adultery can exist in one's heart, so, too, murder can exist in one's heart: "Any one who hates his brother," writes John, "is a murderer" (1 John 3:15).

Violence is not just physical but mental as well. Within ourselves, if we pay attention, there are almost continuous prosecutions conducted "behind closed doors."

I said that in some English translations of the beatitudes, we find the word *gentle* instead of *meek*. There is a nuance about meekness in that word that is important to understand. Saint Paul made this recommendation to the Christians at Philippi: "Let all men know your forbearance" (Philippians 4:5). The Greek word that is translated "forbearance" indicates a whole conglomeration of attitudes that range from clemency to the ability to yield and to show oneself friendly, tolerant and welcoming. This is not far from what we mean today by "gentleness."

It is necessary first of all to rediscover the human value of this virtue. Gentleness is a virtue at risk even of extinction in the society in which we live. Gratuitous violence in films and television, deliberately vulgar language and the competition to push beyond the limits of the tolerable in public venues in terms of violence and explicit sex have accustomed us to all kinds of expressions of brutality and vulgarity.

Gentleness is a balm in human relations. I am convinced that people would be much happier in families if they were a bit gentler in their actions, in their words and above all in their hearts. Nothing spoils the joy of being together as much as rough treatment.

A soft answer turns away wrath,
    but a harsh word stirs up anger. (Proverbs 15:1)

A gentle tongue is a tree of life. (Proverbs 15:4)

A pleasant voice multiples friends and softens enemies,
    and a gracious tongue multiples courtesies. (Sirach 6:5)

A gentle person leaves behind a wave of affection and admiration wherever he or she goes. "What a nice person!" is the first thing others say as soon as he or she is out of earshot.

In addition to the human value of this virtue, we need to rediscover the gospel value of gentleness, which goes beyond a good upbringing and good manners. In the Bible the words *meek* and *gentle* do not convey a passive meaning of "submissive" but rather a sense of someone acting with respect, courtesy and mercy toward others.

Paul places gentleness among the fruits of the Spirit when he says that the fruit of the Spirit is "love, joy, peace, patience, kindness, goodness, faithfulness, gentleness, self-control" (Galatians 5:22–23). For Saint Thomas Aquinas, gentleness is one of the characteristics of charity. It does not exclude righteous anger, but it is able to moderate anger in a way that does not prevent a person from evaluating circumstances with peace and justice. The clearest sign of its presence is that we respectfully acknowledge whoever is before us as a human being, with his or her sensitivity and dignity, and that we do not consider ourselves superior.

Putting on the Meekness of Christ

One more observation before concluding. By their nature the beatitudes are oriented toward practice. They call for imitation and emphasize action on the part of a human being. There is the risk that a person could be discouraged because of experiencing an inability to live them out and because of the great gulf that exists between the ideal and the practice. It could be useful here to recall the purpose that Luther assigned the beatitudes: to force the sinner to recognize his or her powerlessness and to appropriate the virtues of Christ.

The beatitudes, as I said, are the self-portrait of Jesus. He has lived them all to the highest degree. However—and here is the good news—he did not live them only for himself but for all of us. Through the beatitudes we are called not only to imitation but also to appropriation. By faith we can draw on the meekness of Christ, just as we can draw on his purity of heart and every other virtue of his. We can pray to have meekness the way Augustine prayed to have chastity: "You enjoin meekness: give what you command, and command what you will."[20]

"Put on then, as God's chosen ones, holy and beloved, compassion, kindness, lowliness, meekness [*prautes*], and patience," writes Paul (Colossians 3:12). Kindness and meekness are like a robe that Christ has won for us and with which, by faith, we can clothe ourselves. This is not, of course, so that we can dispense from the practice of meekness but to encourage us in it. *Prautes* (meekness, gentleness) is listed by Paul with the fruits of the Spirit in Galatians 5:23 because it is among the qualities that a believer demonstrates in his or her life when he or she receives the Spirit of Christ and tries to respond to it.

We can end, then, confidently reciting together the beautiful invocation from the litany of the Sacred Heart: "Jesus, meek and humble of heart, make our hearts like yours": *Jesu, mitis et humilis corde, fac cor nostrum secundum cor tuum.*

Chapter Four

BLESSED ARE YOU WHO HUNGER NOW, FOR YOU SHALL BE SATISFIED

History and Spirit

The research on the historical Jesus that is so fashionable today—whether by scholarly believers or by some nonbelievers doing farfetched study—conceals a grave danger: It can lead people to believe that something is authentic only when it can be traced back to the earthly Jesus; everything else is considered nonhistorical and thus not authentic. This would mean unfairly limiting to history the ways that God has at his disposal to reveal himself. It would mean tacitly abandoning the truth of faith in biblical inspiration and thus the revelatory character of Scripture.

The Word of God, which is normative for the believer, does not consist in some kind of hypothetical original nucleus variously reconstructed by historians; the Word of God is what is written in the Gospels. The result of historical research should be held in great esteem because it is needed to guide our understanding of subsequent developments in tradition. However, we will continue to exclaim, "The Gospel of the Lord!" at the end of a reading from the Gospel—but not at the end of a reading from the latest book about the historical Jesus.

These two ways of interpreting, from history and from faith, have an important point of intersection. According to an eminent New Testament scholar, "An historical 'event' is an occurrence *plus* the interest and meaning which the occurrence possessed for the persons involved in it, and by which the record is determined."[1] An infinite number of facts have actually occurred that we would never dream of calling historical because they have left no trace in history; they have generated no interest whatsoever and have brought forth nothing new. *Historical*, then, does not refer only to the bare, plain facts of an account but to the *fact* plus its *significance*.

This means that the Gospels are historical not just because they relate what actually happened but also because of the significance of those facts, which is brought to light by the Holy Spirit's inspiration. The Gospel writers and the apostolic community before them, with their additions and diverse emphases, bring to light a variety of meanings or implications about a particular fact or saying of Jesus. What they bring to light, though, is only some of what the fact or saying potentially means, since the evaluation by the Fathers about the "inexhaustible depth" of revealed Scripture should be attributed in the highest degree to the words of Christ.[2]

John is concerned that this be explained in advance by Jesus himself when he attributes these words to him: "I have yet many things to say to you, but you cannot bear them now.

When the Spirit of truth comes, he will guide you into all the truth; for he will not speak on his own authority, but whatever he hears he will speak, and he will declare to you the things that are to come" (John 16:12–13). This is the perennial problem of the connection between history and spirit. History without spirit is silent; spirit without history is blind.

It seems that a desire not to limit research on the New Testament to history is beginning to gain momentum among various biblical scholars who combine historical and philological exegesis with what is called canonical exegesis, that is, exegesis that takes into account the canon of Scripture and the theological value that is derived from it.

Who Are the Hungry and the Satisfied?

The observations above are particularly useful when dealing with how to make use of the Gospel beatitudes. Let's go back to the fact that the beatitudes have come down to us in two different versions. Matthew has eight beatitudes, and Luke has only four, followed by four contrasting "woes." In Matthew the discourse is indirect: "Blessed are the poor.... Blessed are those who hunger"; in Luke the discourse is direct: "Blessed are you poor.... Blessed are you that hunger now." Matthew speaks of "the poor in spirit" and of those who "hunger and thirst for righteousness"; Luke speaks of the "poor" and "those who hunger." One could say that the geographical setting also reflects this different perspective: Matthew, who spiritualizes the discourse more, places it high above, on a mountain (see Matthew 5:1); Luke, who is more mindful of what happens on earth, locates it below, on a plain (see Luke 6:17).

After all the critical work done to distinguish what goes back to the historical Jesus in the beatitudes and what instead belongs to Matthew and Luke, the believer's task today is not to choose one of the two versions as authentic and to put aside the other. We need instead to receive the message contained in each Gospel version and to emphasize one or the other perspective from time to time, depending on today's circumstances and needs, just as each of the two Gospel writers did in his day.

Following this principle, let us reflect today on the beatitude about those who hunger, starting with the version from Luke: "Blessed are you that hunger now, for you shall be satisfied" (Luke 6:21). (We will see subsequently that Matthew's version of "hungering for righteousness" is not opposed to Luke's version but confirms and reinforces it.) In hearing this beatitude proclaimed, many people react indignantly: How can the hungry be called blessed in a world in which there are millions of people, including children, who die of hunger, while others stuff themselves so much that they ruin their health and others throw tons of food in the garbage?

This indignation is more than justified and is shared by Jesus himself, who pronounces a "woe" immediately following this beatitude: "Woe to you that are full now, for you shall hunger" (Luke 6:25). Jesus tells the parable of the rich man who feasted every day and of Lazarus the beggar (see Luke 16:19–31) precisely to denounce this situation that is evidently not new in the world, although it is occurring today on a global scale. In the Lucan beatitude Jesus says, "Blessed are those who hunger and thirst, *because they shall be satisfied*; woe to you who are full now *because you will hunger*." That same conclusion is present in the parable in a narrative key: "The poor man died and was carried by angels to Abraham's bosom; the rich man also died and was buried... [and went to] Hades" (Luke 16:22–23).

The hungry in Luke's beatitude are not in a different category than the poor who are mentioned in his first beatitude. They are the same people, considered now in the more dramatic aspect of their condition: their lack of food. On the other hand, the "satisfied" are the rich who, in their prosperity, are able to satisfy not only their need for food but also their pleasure in eating abundantly.

The parable of the rich man also looks at poverty and wealth from the perspective of the lack and the overabundance of food. The rich man "feasted sumptuously every day" (Luke 16:19); the beggar longed in vain "to be fed with what fell from the rich man's table" (Luke 16:21). The contrast continues but is reversed in the afterlife: Lazarus once wanted to be fed with the scraps from the table of the rich man, but now it is the rich man who begs Lazarus for a few drops of water to quench his thirst.

This parable, however, not only identifies who the hungry and the satisfied are but also tells us *why* the hungry are called blessed and the others unfortunate. The rich man in this parable and all the other rich people Jesus speaks about in the Gospels are not condemned simply for being rich but because of the use they make, or do not make, of their wealth and because of what wealth produces in them.

Wealth and the satisfactions it can bring tend to keep people tied to an earthly mentality, because "where your treasure is, there will your heart be also" (Luke 12:34). Wealth and satiety weigh people down "with dissipation and drunkenness" (Luke 21:34), choking the seed of the word in them (see Luke 8:14). They make people forget that they could be called upon that very night to give an account of their lives (see Luke 12:16–20). The rich man is unfortunate because his wealth makes his entrance into the kingdom more difficult than a camel's passage "through the eye of a needle" (Luke 18:25).

In the parable of the rich man, Jesus makes clear that there is a way of escape for him: He could remember Lazarus at his door and share his lavish meal with him. The remedy is to make friends of the poor by means of one's wealth, to invite "the poor, the maimed, the lame, the blind" to dinner (Luke 14:13). Satiety, though, dulls a person's spirit and makes it extremely difficult to follow this path. (The story of Zacchaeus proves that it can happen, however rare that may be.) This explains why the "woe" is addressed to the rich and the satisfied, but it is a "woe" that is also born of love and that, rather than being a curse, is a warning to beware!

The best comment on the beatitude of the poor and the hungry is by Mary in the Magnificat: "He has filled the hungry with good things, / and the rich he has sent empty away"

(Luke 1:53). With a series of powerful verbs in the aorist tense, Mary describes a reversal and radical shift in people's standings: "He has scattered,...he has exalted,...he has filled,...he has sent empty away" (Luke 1:51– 53). This is something that has already happened and that happens repeatedly through the action of God.

If we look at history, there does not seem to have been a social revolution in which all of a sudden the rich were impoverished and the hungry were satisfied with food. However, a reversal has come by faith! The kingdom of God has been revealed, and this has brought about a silent but radical revolution. It is as if a new precious element has suddenly been discovered that has devalued monetary currency. The rich man has set aside a considerable sum of money, but during the night a 100 percent devaluation has occurred, and when he rises in the morning he is a miserable pauper. The poor and the hungry, on the contrary, now have an advantage because they are better prepared to accept the new state of affairs. They do not fear the change; they have ready hearts.

Saint James, addressing the rich, says, "Come now, you rich, weep and howl for the miseries that are coming upon you. Your riches have rotted" (James 5:1–2). Here, too, there is nothing that attests that at the time of Saint James the food supply of the rich was rotting in their barns. The apostle means that something has happened that has made these things lose all their value; a new kind of wealth has been revealed. "God [has] chosen those who are poor in the world to be rich in faith and heirs of the kingdom" (James 2:5).

The Magnificat, rather than being an incitement to put down the mighty from their thrones and exalt those of low degree, as it has sometimes been interpreted, is a helpful admonition to the rich and powerful about the tremendous risk they are running, exactly like the "woe" Jesus proclaims and the parable of the rich man.

A Contemporary Parable

A reflection on the beatitude about those who hunger and those who are satisfied is not complete with just an explanation of the exegetical significance of the text and its context. It must also help us to understand the current situation around us and to react to it in the way required by the gospel.

The parable of the rich man and Lazarus the beggar is being repeated today on a global scale. The two characters represent two hemispheres: the rich man represents the Northern Hemisphere (Western Europe, America, Japan); Lazarus the beggar is, with few exceptions, the Southern Hemisphere. Two people, two worlds—the First World and the Third World. Two worlds of unequal size: What we call the Third World actually represents two-thirds of the world!

Someone has compared the earth to a spaceship in flight in which one of the three astronauts on board is consuming 85 percent of the resources on the ship and is plotting to secure the remaining 15 percent as well. Waste is a natural companion for this kind of vast consumption. A few years ago a survey conducted by the United States Department of Agriculture calculated that of the 355 billion pounds of food produced, 87 billion pounds, or about one-fourth, end up in the garbage. We could easily salvage, if we wanted to, about 4.4 billion pounds of this food that is thrown out, a quantity sufficient to feed four million people every year.

The biggest sin against the poor and the hungry is perhaps indifference, making believe we do not see, passing by on the other side of the street (see Luke 10:31). Ignoring "the immense multitudes of the hungry, the needy, the homeless, those without medical care and, above all, those without hope of a better future," writes John Paul II in his encyclical *Sollicitudo Rei Socialis*, would mean "becoming like the 'rich man' who pretended not to know the beggar Lazarus lying at his gate."[3]

We tend to put up insulated windows between ourselves and the poor. The effect of insulated windows, so widely used today, is to keep out the cold and noise; they temper everything, cushioning and muffling disturbances. We see the poor moving around, agitated, crying out from the television screen and the pages of newspapers and missionary magazines, but their cry reaches us as though from a great distance. It does not reach our hearts, or it reaches them only for a moment.

The first thing to do on behalf of the poor, then, is to smash the "insulated windows," to overcome the indifference and insensitivity, to lay aside our defenses and allow ourselves to be invaded by a healthy unease because of the dreadful misery that is in the world. We are called to share in the sighing of Christ: "I have compassion on the crowd, because they... have nothing to eat" (Mark 8:2). When someone has the opportunity to visit villages in certain African countries and to see in person what misery and hunger are like—not on paper but in reality—then this is not difficult.

To eliminate or reduce the unjust and scandalous gulf that exists between the satisfied and the hungry of the world is the most urgent and enormous task that the old millennium has left to the new. It is a task in which especially all religions should take the lead and be united rather than competitive. Such a gigantic undertaking cannot be promoted by political leaders or powers, because these are biased in the interest of their own nations and often by strong economic forces.

Pope Benedict XVI gave us an example of promoting this undertaking with the strong appeal he addressed to the diplomatic corps assigned to the Holy See: "Among the key issues, how can we not think of the millions of people, especially women and children, who lack water, food, or shelter? The worsening scandal of hunger is unacceptable in a world which has the resources, the knowledge, and the means available to bring it to an end."[4]

Technology allows us today to exchange all kinds of information in real time with no barriers, even between the First and Third Worlds, but it shows itself ineffective when it comes to exchanging the products that are the most indispensable for life, food.

"Blessed Are Those Who Hunger and Thirst for Righteousness"
I said at the beginning that the two versions of the beatitudes

about those who hunger, Luke's and Matthew's, are not opposed but complement each other. Matthew does not speak of physical hunger but of hunger and thirst "for righteousness." There are two basic interpretations for his phrase. The first, in line with Lutheran theology, interprets this beatitude in the light of what Saint Paul will later say about righteousness through faith. To hunger and thirst for righteousness means to be aware of one's own need for righteousness and of an inability to acquire it on one's own through works and thus to humbly wait for it from God. In the other interpretation righteousness is "not what God himself performs or grants but rather what he requires from human beings, i.e., what merits, as it did for Joseph, the title of 'righteous man.'"[5]

In the light of this second interpretation, which is by far the most common and the most valid exegetically, the physical hunger in Luke and the spiritual hunger in Matthew no longer seem unrelated. Championing the hungry and the poor belong to the category of works of righteousness and will in fact be, according to Matthew, the basic criteria used at the end of time to separate the righteous and the unrighteous (see Matthew 25:31–46).

The righteousness God requires of human beings is summarized in the dual precept of love of God and love of neighbor (see Matthew 22:37–40). It is love of neighbor, then, that should motivate those who hunger for righteousness to care for those who hunger for bread. This is the great principle by which the gospel operates in the sphere of social action.

Liberal theology has been correct on this point, as we can see in the words of one of its most illustrious representatives, Adolph von Harnack:

> [T]he Gospel nowhere teaches that our relations to the brethren should be characterized by a holy indifference. Such indifference expresses rather what the individual soul should feel towards the world with all its weal and woe. Whenever it is a question of one's neighbour, the Gospel will not hear of this indifference, but, on the contrary, preaches always love and mercy. Further, the Gospel regards as absolutely inseparable the temporal and spiritual needs of the brethren.[6]

The gospel does not encourage the hungry to get justice or to rise up on their own because in Jesus' time—although not the case today—they had no theoretical or practical means to do so. The gospel does not ask them for the useless sacrifice of getting themselves killed by following some zealous rabble-rouser or homegrown Spartacus. Jesus challenges the strong, not the weak. He himself confronts the ire and the sarcasm of the rich with his "woes" (see Luke 16:14–15) and does not leave that for the victims to do.

To try to find in the Gospels, no matter how, models and explicit invitations to the poor and the hungry to reverse their situation themselves is fruitless and anachronistic, and it loses sight of the real contribution that the Gospels can bring to their cause. Rudolf Bultmann is right about this when he writes, "Christianity is quite uninterested in making the world a better place, it has no proposals for political or social reform"[7]—even though his statement needs qualification.

The beatitudes are not the only way of confronting the problem of wealth and poverty, of hunger and satisfaction. There are other ways due to the development of a social consciousness that has emerged during the course of history, not necessarily from faith. Christians rightly give their support to these other ways, and the church in its social teaching supports them with its discernment.

The great message of the beatitudes is that, regardless of what the rich and the satisfied will or will not do concerning the current status of things, the situation of the poor and of those who hunger for righteousness is preferable to that of the rich. There are levels and aspects of reality that do not appear to the naked eye except with the help of special light, like infrared and ultraviolet light. These are used quite a bit in satellite photography. A picture obtained with this light is quite different and surprising for those who are used to seeing that same panorama in natural light. The beatitudes are a kind of infrared light: They give us a different picture of reality, the really true one, because they show what will remain at the end when the "form of this world" has passed away (1 Corinthians 7:31).

Physical Bread and Eucharistic Bread

Jesus has left us a perfect antithesis of the banquet of the rich man, the Eucharist. It is the daily celebration of a great banquet to which the master invites the "poor and maimed and blind and lame" (Luke 14:21), that is, all the poor Lazaruses who are in the vicinity. The Eucharist is the perfect "communal banquet": the same food and drink, in the same quantity, for all—for the one who presides as well as for the newest arrival to the community, for the richest as well as the poorest.

The link between physical and spiritual bread was very visible in the early days of the church, when the Lord's Supper, called an *agape*, occurred within the framework of a communal meal, in which people shared bread as well as the Eucharist. Saint Paul wrote to the Corinthians who had acted inappropriately in this regard, "When you meet together, it is not the Lord's supper that you eat. For in eating, each one goes ahead with his own meal, and one is hungry and another is drunk" (1 Corinthians 11:20–21). This is a very serious accusation, as if he is saying, "Your meal is not a Eucharist anymore!"

Today the Eucharist is no longer celebrated in the context of a shared meal, but the contrast between those who have an abundance and those who do not have even the bare necessities has assumed global dimensions, even among Christians. The recent post-synodal exhortation on the Eucharist makes that point forcefully: "The food of truth demands that we denounce inhumane situations in which people starve to death because of injustice and exploitation, and it gives us renewed strength and courage to work tirelessly in the service of the civilization of love."[8]

In rich countries everywhere the Catholic church supports national and diocesan Caritas groups, soup kitchens and initiatives for feeding people in developing countries. One of the signs of vitality of our religious communities, and of new ecclesial movements as well, is that soup kitchens exist in almost all our cities and distribute thousands of meals daily in an atmosphere of respect and hospitality. It is a drop in the ocean of poverty, but even the ocean, as Mother Teresa of Calcutta used to say, is made up of many small drops.

I would like to end with the prayer that we recite every day in our Capuchin community before a meal: "Lord, bless this food that we are about to receive from your bounty, help us to provide for those who do not have any, and make us participants one day in your heavenly banquet, through Christ our Lord."

Chapter Five

BLESSED ARE THE MERCIFUL, FOR THEY SHALL OBTAIN MERCY

The Mercy of Christ

The fifth beatitude in Matthew is "Blessed are the merciful, for they shall obtain mercy" (5:7). Keeping in mind that the beatitudes are the self-portrait of Christ, we can start by asking this time as well, "How did Jesus live out mercy? What does his life tell us about this beatitude?"

In the Bible the word *mercy* (*hesed*) has two fundamental meanings. The first indicates the attitude of the stronger party (in the covenant, God himself) toward the weaker party and is usually expressed by forgiveness for unfaithfulness and sins. The second meaning indicates the attitude toward the need and suffering—not necessarily the sin—of the other and is expressed in what we call works of mercy. There is, so to speak, a mercy of the heart and a mercy of hands.

In Jesus' life both of these forms of mercy shine forth. He reflects the mercy of God toward sinners, but he is also moved to compassion for all human suffering and need: He takes action to feed the crowd, to heal the sick, to set the oppressed free. The Gospel writer says of him, "He took our infirmities and bore our diseases" (Matthew 8:17; see Isaiah 53:4).

The primary meaning of *mercy* in this beatitude is certainly the first, that of the forgiveness and remission of sins. We can assume this from the connection between the beatitude and its reward: "Blessed are the merciful, for they shall obtain mercy" points to the mercy of God, who will remit their sins. The statement "Be merciful, even as your Father is merciful" (Luke 6:36) is immediately clarified in the next verse by this parallel: "Forgive, and you will be forgiven" (v. 37).

Everyone knows the welcome that Jesus affords sinners in the Gospels and the opposition that it provokes on the part of the defenders of the Law, who accuse him of being "a glutton and a drunkard, a friend of tax collectors and sinners!" (Luke 7:34). One of the best historically attested sayings of Jesus is "I came not to call the righteous, but sinners" (Mark 2:17). Feeling themselves accepted by him and not judged, sinners listen to him willingly.

But who were the sinners? What is meant by this word?

In line with a widespread tendency today to clear the Pharisees entirely by attributing their negative image to a later twisting by the Gospel writers, someone has maintained that *sinners* refers to the people who "were deliberate and unrepentant transgressors of the law."[1] In other words, *sinners* would refer to the ordinary delinquents and lawbreakers of that time. If this were the case, the adversaries of Jesus would actually have had a reason for being scandalized and for thinking of him as an irresponsible and socially dangerous person. It would be as if a priest today habitually spent time with the Mafia, with organized gangs or with criminals in general and accepted their invitations to dinner on the pretext of talking to them about God.

This is not the way things really were. The Pharisees had their own vision of the Law and of what conformed to or contradicted it, and they considered as reprobates all those who did not conform to their practices. Jesus does not deny that sin and sinners exist; he does not justify the fraud of Zacchaeus or the adultery of the woman. The fact that he refers to them as "those who are sick" (Mark 2:17) proves that. What Jesus condemns is people's establishing what true righteousness is on their own and considering everyone else "thieves, unrighteous, and adulterers" (Luke 18:11), denying even the possibility of their changing.

The way Luke introduces the parable of the Pharisee and the publican is revealing: "He also told this parable to some who trusted in themselves that they were righteous and despised others" (Luke 18:9). According to one exegete, "Jesus, in other words, was more critical of those who dismissively condemned 'sinners' than of the sinners themselves."[2]

A God Who Delights in Showing Mercy

Jesus justifies his conduct toward sinners, saying that this is the way his heavenly Father acts. He reminds those who oppose him of the word of God in the prophets: "I desire mercy, and not sacrifice" (Matthew 9:13; see Hosea 6:6). Mercy toward the unfaithfulness of the people, *hesed*, is the most salient characteristic of the God of the covenant and fills the Bible from beginning to end. One psalm repeats it like a litany and uses it to explain all the events of Israel's history: "For his mercy endures for ever" (Psalm 136).

Therefore, being merciful seems to be an essential quality for a human being if he or she is to be in the image and likeness of God (see Genesis 1:26). "Be merciful, even as your Father is merciful" (Luke 6:36) is a paraphrase of the famous verse, "You shall be holy; for I the LORD your God am holy" (Leviticus 19:2).

The most surprising thing about God's mercy is that he experiences joy in having mercy. Jesus concludes the parable of the lost sheep by saying, "There will be more joy in heaven over one sinner who repents than over ninety-nine righteous persons who need no repentance" (Luke 15:7). The woman who found the lost coin cries out to her friends, "Rejoice with me" (Luke 15:9). In the parable of the prodigal son, joy overflows and becomes a feast, a banquet (see Luke 15:11–32).

This is not an isolated theme in the Bible but is instead profoundly rooted there. In Ezekiel God says, "I have no pleasure in the death of the wicked, but [I take pleasure!] that the wicked turn from his way and live" (33:11). Micah says that God "*delights* in mercy" (Micah 7:18, emphasis added), that he experiences pleasure in showing mercy.

But why, we can ask, should one sheep count as much as all the remaining sheep put together, and the one that counts most should be the one that has gotten lost and created the most problems?

I have found a convincing explanation in the poet Charles Péguy: being lost, this sheep, like the younger son, made God's heart tremble. God feared losing him forever, being forced to condemn him and to be deprived of him for eternity. This fear caused hope to arise in God, and once that hope was realized, it resulted in joy and feasting. "And this [person's] very repentance / Was for him [God]...the crowning of a hope."[3] Péguy is using figurative language, like all our language about God, but it conveys a truth.

For human beings, what makes hope possible is the fact that we do not know the future and therefore we hope. For God, who knows the future, what makes hope possible is that he does not want to—and in a certain sense cannot—bring to pass what he wants without our consent. The free will of human beings explains the existence of hope in God.

What can we say then about the ninety-nine righteous sheep and the elder brother? Is there no joy in heaven over them? Is there any point to living one's whole life as a good Christian?

Let us recall what the Father said to the elder brother: "Son, you are always with me, and all that is mine is yours" (Luke 15:31). The error of the elder son is in thinking that staying at home and sharing everything with the Father is something he deserves rather than an immense privilege. He is acting more like a mercenary than a son. This should put on notice all of us who, because of our state in life, find ourselves in the same position as the elder son!

On this point reality is better than the parable. In reality the elder brother—the Firstborn of the Father, the Word—did not remain in his Father's house. He is the one who went to a "far country" (see Luke 15:13) to find the younger son, that is, fallen humanity. It is he who led him back home; it is he who procured new clothes for him and prepared a banquet for him, to which he can come in every Eucharist.

In one of his novels, Dostoevsky describes a scene that seems like something he might have actually observed. A peasant woman is holding her baby, who is a few weeks old when, according to her, he smiles at her for the first time. Very soberly she makes the Sign of the Cross, and when she is asked about that gesture she answers, "There is joy for a mother in her child's first smile, just as God rejoices when from heaven he sees a sinner praying to him with his whole heart."[4]

Our Mercy: Cause or Effect of God's Mercy?
Jesus says, "Blessed are the merciful, *for they shall obtain mercy*," and he tells us to pray in the Our Father, "Forgive us our trespasses, *as we forgive those who trespass against us*." He also says, "If you do not forgive men their trespasses, neither will your Father forgive your trespasses" (Matthew 6:12, 15, emphasis added).

These statements could lead us to believe that God's mercy toward us is the result of our mercy toward others and is proportionate to it. If this were the case, however, the relationship between grace and good works would be com-

pletely turned upside down, and the purely gratuitous character of divine mercy that God solemnly proclaimed to Moses
would be destroyed: "I will be gracious to whom I will be gracious, and will show mercy on whom I will show mercy"
(Exodus 33:19).

The parable of the unmerciful servant (see Matthew
18:23–34) is the key to correctly interpreting the relationship. We see there how the master, taking the initiative and
without conditions, forgives his servant an immense debt
(ten thousand talents!). And it is precisely his generosity that
should move this servant to have pity on the one who owes
him the paltry sum of a hundred denarii.

We should have mercy, then, *because* we have received
mercy and not *in order to* receive mercy. We need to have
mercy since otherwise the mercy of God will not be effective
for us and will be withdrawn, as the master in the parable
withdraws it from his unmerciful servant. Grace always
comes first, and it is what creates our obligation to respond:
"As the Lord has forgiven you, so you also must forgive,"
writes Paul to the Colossians (3:13).

If God's mercy toward us in the beatitude seems to be the
result of our mercy toward our brothers and sisters, it is
because Jesus is speaking about mercy here from the perspective of the final judgment. ("They shall obtain mercy" in
the future!) Saint James writes, in fact, that "judgment is
without mercy to one who has shown no mercy; yet mercy tri-
umphs over judgment" (James 2:13).

Experiencing Divine Mercy

If divine mercy is at the beginning of this cycle, and it requires and makes possible mercy to one another, then the most important thing is for us to have a renewed experience of the mercy of God.

Franz Kafka's novel *The Trial* is about a man who is arrested one day, without anyone knowing why, although he is allowed to continue his solitary life and his modest job as a clerk. He begins an extensive investigation to understand the reasons, the court, the accusations and the procedure. But no one knows what to tell him except that there really is a prosecution underway against him. Finally one day they take him away to execute his sentence, death.

In the course of the story, it becomes clear that there are three possibilities for this man: a definite acquittal, an apparent acquittal and a postponement. An apparent acquittal and a postponement would resolve nothing; they would only keep the accused in a state of uncertainty for the rest of his life. Instead, "in definite acquittal the documents relating to the case are said to be completely annulled, they simply vanish from sight, not only the charge but also the records of the case and even the acquittal are destroyed, everything is destroyed."[5]

But no one is sure if definite acquittals, which people long for, really exist. There are only rumors about them, only "wonderful legends." The novel finishes this way, like all this author's works: A solution is seen from afar, and the character chases after it breathlessly without any possibility

EIGHT STEPS TO HAPPINESS

of attaining it, just as in nightmares.

The Word of God tells us the amazing news that a "definite acquittal" exists for human beings; it is not just a very wonderful but unattainable legend. Jesus has destroyed "the bond which stood against us with its legal demands; this he set aside, nailing it to the cross" (Colossians 2:14). He has completely destroyed it. "There is...now no condemnation for those who are in Christ Jesus," Paul proclaims (Romans 8:1). No condemnation! Of any kind! For those who believe in Christ Jesus!

In Jerusalem there was a miraculous pool, and the first person who was lowered into it when the water was stirred was healed (see John 5:2–9). The reality is infinitely greatly than the symbol here as well. From the cross of Christ a fountain of water and blood sprang forth, and not just one person but all who immerse themselves in it will emerge healed.

After baptism this miraculous pool is the sacrament of reconciliation. At times it is good to make a "nonroutine" confession—one that is different from the habitual confession —in which we really allow the Paraclete to convict us of sin (see John 16:8).

There is a special grace when not just an individual but the whole community comes before God in this penitential attitude. After a profound experience of the mercy of God, people come out renewed and full of hope: "God, who is rich in mercy, out of the great love with which he loved us, even when we were dead through our trespasses, *made us alive together with Christ*" (Ephesians 2:4–5, emphasis added).

A Church "Rich in Mercy"

After experiencing God's mercy, we should in turn extend that to our brothers and sisters, especially as the church. Preaching the spiritual exercises to the Roman Curia in the jubilee year of 2000, Cardinal Francis Xavier Van Thuan, alluding to the rite of the opening of the Holy Door, said in a meditation, "I dream of a church that is the *Holy Door*, always open, embracing all, full of compassion; and that understands the pain and sufferings of humanity, protecting and consoling all people."[6]

The church of the God who is "rich in mercy," *dives in misericordia*, cannot be other than *dives in misericordia* as well. We can understand what that means from Christ's attitude toward sinners discussed above. He does not trivialize sin yet finds a way of never alienating sinners but rather of drawing them to himself. He sees in them not only what they are but also what they can become if divine mercy reaches them in the depths of their misery and desperation. He does not wait for them to come to him; he often seeks them out himself.

Today most exegetes agree that Jesus did not have a hostile attitude toward the Mosaic Law and that he himself scrupulously observed it. What put him in conflict with the religious *élite* of his time was a certain rigid and sometimes inhuman manner in which they interpreted the Law. "The sabbath was made for man," he said, "not man for the sabbath" (Mark 2:27), and what he says about Sabbath rest, one of the most sacred laws in Israel, applies to all the other laws.

Jesus is firm and rigorous about his principles, but he

knows when any given principle needs to yield to a higher one, like the mercy of God and the salvation of human beings. The way these criteria derived from Christ's action can be applied to the concrete problems of our current time (abortion, divorce, euthanasia) depends on patient study and ultimately on the discernment of the magisterium. In the life of the church, however, as in the life of Jesus, both the mercy of the heart and the mercy of hands should shine forth together, whether it be "visceral mercy" or works of mercy.

"Put on. . .Compassion"

The last word on every beatitude must always be one that touches us personally and motivates each of us to conversion and action. Saint Paul exhorted the Colossians with these heartfelt words:

> Put on then, as God's chosen ones, holy and beloved, compassion [literally "viscera"], kindness, lowliness, meekness, and patience, forbearing one another and, if one has a complaint against another, forgiving each other; as the Lord has forgiven you, so you also must forgive. (Colossians 3:12–13)

Saint Augustine says, "We are mortal human beings, fragile, weak, carrying along with us our earthen vessels, which don't leave each other much room."[7] We cannot live together in harmony, in a family or in another kind of community, without the practice of forgiveness and reciprocal mercy. Mercy (*misericordia*) is a word that comes from *misereo* and *cor*, and it means to have one's heart moved by pity, to be moved emotionally, with regard to the suffering or the mis-take of a brother or sister. This is how God explains his mercy when he sees his people going astray: "My heart is over-whelmed, / my pity is stirred" (Hosea 11:8, *NAB*).

We need to respond with forgiveness and even, when pos-sible, with excusing others instead of condemning them. Regarding ourselves this saying applies: "He who excuses himself, God accuses; he who accuses himself, God excuses." Regarding others the converse applies: "He who excuses his brother is excused by God; he who accuses his brother is accused by God."

Forgiveness does for a community what oil does for a motor. If someone begins a trip in a car without one drop of oil in the engine, after a few minutes the whole car will be on fire. Like oil, forgiveness neutralizes friction.

The oil that we need to pour into the gears of life consists above all in kind words. The apostle exhorted the Ephesians this way about it: "Let no evil talk come out of your mouths, but only such as is good for edifying, as fits the occasion, that it may impart grace to those who hear" (Ephesians 4:29). A kind word—a positive word of encouragement or praise—is a balm, especially in a family situation.

Mercy toward one another should be the most natural sen-timent for human beings. The poet Charles Péguy puts these words in God's mouth:

Charity, said God, does not surprise me.

. . .

> These poor creatures are so wretched that unless they have
> Hearts of stone, why would they not love each other [?][8]

To avoid having even a little compassion, we would need to close our eyes and ears to the cry of desolation that reaches us from all sides.

This is perhaps the clearest intersection point between Christianity and Buddhism. In Buddhism compassion for every living creature is what constitutes "right action" and is one of the steps of the "noble eightfold path" that brings a person to illumination. However, the motivation is different in these two religious worlds. In Christianity the basis is that the human being is created in the image of a God who is "the Father of mercies and God of all comfort" (2 Corinthians 1:3). Wisdom says of God, "You love all things that exist, / and you loathe none of the things which you have made" (Wisdom 11:24). In Buddhism, which does not acknowledge the idea of a personal God and creator, the basis is anthropological and cosmic: Human beings should be merciful because of the solidarity and the responsibility that links them to all living things.

This difference, however, should not prevent us from acting together on a practical level, especially today when life is so threatened with violence and when relationships have become so bitter and cutthroat. We Christians can learn much from the books of the current Dalai Lama, Tenzin Gyatso, that propose an "ethic of peace and compassion"[9] for the third millennium. From every page the books exude a great sense of solidarity and almost of tenderness toward all living things and suggest how to transfer this vision into politics, economics and all other areas of life.

Earth would be a much more livable place if we learned to think a little more about the misfortunes and the sufferings of others and a little less exclusively about ourselves—if we learned to substitute a genuine compassion for our neighbor for our own self-pity. Jesus said, "Blessed are the merciful, for they shall obtain mercy." They will find it not only with God, in the final judgment, but also here on earth now with their fellow creatures.

I have used the image of oil. Psalm 133 sings of the goodness and joy of living together in harmony: it says that it is "like the precious oil upon the head" that runs down Aaron's beard and vestments (Psalm 133:2). Our Aaron, our high priest, is Christ; mercy and forgiveness comprise the oil that runs down this "head" lifted up on the cross and spreads down through the body of the church to the hem of his vestments, to those who live at its margins.

Let us try, concretely, to identify among our relationships the person who seems to us the most in need of having the oil of mercy and reconciliation, and let us pour it out on that person, silently and abundantly. The psalm concludes by saying that wherever people live in forgiveness and reciprocal mercy, "there the LORD has commanded the blessing, / life for evermore" (Psalm 133:3).

Chapter Six

BLESSED ARE THE PURE IN HEART, FOR THEY SHALL SEE GOD

From Ritual Purity to Purity of Heart

Whoever reads or hears proclaimed, "Blessed are the pure in heart, for they shall see God," instinctively thinks today of the virtue of chastity, as though this beatitude is the positive and internalized equivalent of the sixth commandment, "You shall not commit adultery" (Exodus 20:14). This interpretation, periodically advanced throughout the history of Christian spirituality, has been the predominant one since the nineteenth century.

Actually, in Christ's thinking purity of heart does not point to a particular virtue but is a quality that should accompany all the virtues, so that they are truly virtues rather than "splendid vices."[1] The clearest opposite of purity is not impurity but hypocrisy. A bit of exegesis and history will help us to understand this better.

From the context of the Sermon on the Mount, we can clearly infer what Jesus means by "purity of heart." According to the Gospel, what determines the purity or impurity of an action—whether it is giving alms, fasting or prayer—is the intention, that is, whether it is done to be seen by others or to please God: "Thus, when you give alms, sound no trumpet before you, as the hypocrites do in the synagogues and in the streets, that they may be praised by men. Truly, I say to you, they have their reward. But when you give alms, do not let your left hand know what your right hand is doing, so that your alms may be in secret; and your Father who sees in secret will reward you" (Matthew 6:2–4).

Hypocrisy is the sin that God denounces most forcefully throughout the Bible, and the reason is clear. Through hypocrisy people dethrone God and put him in second place while placing creatures—public opinion—in first place. "Man looks on the outward appearance, but the LORD looks on the heart" (1 Samuel 16:7). To focus on appearance more than on the heart means making people more important than God.

Hypocrisy is thus essentially a lack of faith. But it is also a lack of charity toward one's neighbor in the sense that it tends to reduce people to admirers. It does not acknowledge people's dignity but sees them only as a function of one's own image.

The judgment of Christ on hypocrisy is final: "*Receperunt mercedem suam*"—"They have already received their reward!" A reward, moreover, that is illusory even on the human level because glory, as we know, flees from whoever chases it and follows whoever flees from it.

The invectives Jesus pronounces against the scribes and Pharisees also help us understand the meaning of this beatitude about the pure in heart. They all center on the opposition between "from within" and "from without," between internal and external: "Woe to you, scribes and Pharisees, hypocrites! for you are like whitewashed tombs, which outwardly appear beautiful, but within they are full of dead men's bones and all uncleanness. So you also outwardly appear righteous to men, but within you are full of hypocrisy and iniquity" (Matthew 23:27–28).

The revolution accomplished by Jesus in this area is of incalculable importance. There is a tendency today not to emphasize the contrast between Jesus and the Pharisees because of the convergence that exists in their way of relating to the Mosaic Law. Except for an occasional mention of inner purity prior to Christ by the prophets or in the psalms (such as, "Who shall ascend the hill of the LORD? / ... / He who has clean hands and a pure heart" [Psalm 24:3–4]), it is clear that purity was primarily understood in a ritual sense. It consisted in keeping away from things, animals, people or places that were thought to be capable of defiling a person and separating him or her from the holiness of God. In particular, things that are linked to birth, death, food and sexuality fall into this category. In different ways and with different presuppositions, this same approach was taken by nonbiblical religions as well.

Jesus makes a clean sweep of all these taboos. He does so above all through his actions: He eats with sinners, touches lepers, spends time with pagans—all things that were held to be highly defiling. He also does so through the teachings he imparts. The solemnity with which he introduces his discourse on the pure and impure tells us that he is conscious of the novelty of his teaching:

> And he called the people to him again, and said to them, "Hear me, all of you, and understand: there is nothing outside a man which by going into him can defile him; but the things which come out of a man are what defile him.... For from within, out of the heart of man, come evil thoughts, fornication, theft, murder, adultery, coveting, wickedness, deceit, licentiousness, envy, slander, pride, foolishness. All these evil things come from within, and they defile a man." (Mark 7:14–15; 21–23)

The Gospel writer notes, as if with amazement, "Thus he declared all foods clean" (Mark 7:19). The apostolic church, opposing the attempt by some Judeo-Christians to restore the distinction between pure and impure in food and in other areas of life, reasserted strongly, "To the pure all things are pure" (Titus 1:15; see Romans 14:20).

Purity, understood in the sense of continence and chastity, is not absent from this gospel beatitude. (Among the things that defile the heart, Jesus, as we just heard, also adds "fornication, adultery, licentiousness.") However, purity in this sense occupies a limited and secondary place, so to speak. It is like other areas in which the heart plays the decisive role; for example, when Jesus says, "Every one who looks at a woman lustfully has already committed adultery with her in his heart" (Matthew 5:28).

The words *pure* and *purity* (*katharos, katharotïs*) are never actually used in the New Testament to indicate what we mean by them today—the absence of sins of the flesh. Other words were used to convey that meaning: self-control (*enkrateia*), temperance (*sophrosyne*) and chastity (*hagneia*).

As I have said, it is clear, as always, that "the pure in heart" par excellence is Jesus himself. His own adversaries were forced to say about him, "We know that you are true, and care for no man; for you do not regard the position of men, but truly teach the way of God" (Mark 12:14). Jesus could say of himself, "I do not seek my own glory" (John 8:50).

A Look at History

In the exegesis of the Fathers, very early on we see three fundamental directions in which the beatitude about the pure in heart will be understood and interpreted during the history of Christian spirituality: moral, mystical and ascetic. The *moral* interpretation puts the emphasis on right intention; the *mystical* interpretation puts the emphasis on the vision of God; and the *ascetic* interpretation puts the emphasis on the struggle against the passions of the flesh. We see these three exemplified, respectively, in Augustine, Gregory of Nyssa and John Chrysostom.

Augustine, faithfully paying attention to the Gospel context, gives a *moral interpretation* to this beatitude as the rejection of "practicing your piety before men in order to be seen by them" (Matthew 6:1). Thus he sees it as describing the simplicity and honesty that are the opposite of hypocrisy: "No one therefore has a single, i.e., a pure heart," he says, "except the man who rises above the praises of men; and when he lives well, looks only at Him, who is the only Searcher of the conscience."[2]

The deciding factor here about purity or impurity of heart is the intention. Augustine says, "All our works are pure and well-pleasing in the sight of God, when they are done... with a heavenly intent, having that end of love in view.... It is not, therefore, what one does, but the intent with which he does it, that is to be considered."[3] This interpretive model emphasizing intention will remain operative in all the spiritual traditions that follow, especially the Ignatian tradition.

The *mystical interpretation*, promoted by Gregory of Nyssa, interprets the beatitude in terms of contemplation. Everyone must purify his or her heart from every tie with the world and with evil. In so doing a person's heart will become that pure and clear image of God that it was at the beginning, and within his or her own soul, as in a mirror, human beings will be able to "see God": "If... you wash off by a good life the filth that has been stuck on your heart like plaster, the Divine Beauty will again shine forth in you.... Hence, if a man who is pure of heart sees himself, he sees in himself what he desires; and thus he becomes blessed."[4]

Here the focus is wholly on the *apodosis*, on the fruit promised by this beatitude. Having a pure heart is the means, and the end is "to see God." One can note here, on the linguistic level, the influence of the speculation by Plotinus, which is even more evident in Saint Basil.[5]

This line of interpretation will also have followers in the

later history of Christian spirituality, like Saint Bernard, Saint Bonaventure and the Rhine mystics.[6] In some monastic circles an interesting new idea is added, however: Purity brings about the interior unification that occurs when a person wants only one thing, in this case, God. Saint Bernard writes,

> "Blessed are the pure in heart, for they shall see God," as if to say: Purify your heart, free yourself from all things, become a monk—that is, become singular of heart. Seek but one thing from the Lord, ask but for this [see Psalm 27:4].... When you have purified your heart..., you shall soon see God. [see Psalm 46:10][7]

The *ascetic interpretation*—the identification of purity with chastity, which becomes predominant, as I said, beginning in the nineteenth century—is rare in the Fathers and medieval authors. John Chrysostom gives us the clearest example: "'Blessed are the pure in heart, for they shall see God.' Now He here calls 'pure,' either those who have attained unto all virtue, and are not conscious to themselves of any evil; or those who live in temperance. For there is nothing which we need so much in order to see God, as this last virtue."[8]

In keeping with this tradition, the mystic John Ruusbroec distinguishes a chastity of the spirit, a chastity of the heart and a chastity of the body. He connects the gospel beatitude to chastity of heart: "[Purity] guards and protects the external senses, subdues and restrains the lustful desires..., and serves as a lock for the heart by keeping out earthly things and everything deceitful, even as it opens up the heart to heavenly realities and to all truth."[9]

With different degrees of faithfulness, all these orthodox interpretations remain within the new framework of the revolution brought by Jesus in which every moral discussion leads back to the heart. Paradoxically, those who betrayed the gospel beatitude of the pure (*katharoi*) in heart are precisely those who took their name from that word, the Cathari and all the similar movements that preceded and came after them in the history of Christianity. They fall into the category of those who make purity consist in ritual and social separation from people and things that are judged to be impure by nature—a purity that is more external than internal.

We Have Two Lives

We have seen that in Christ's thinking purity of heart is primarily the opposite not of impurity but of hypocrisy, and hypocrisy is the human vice that is perhaps the most widespread and least confessed. We have two lives, wrote Blaise Pascal: One is our true life, and the other is the one that exists in our minds or in the minds of others. We work tirelessly to adorn and preserve our imaginary existence and neglect the real one. If we possess a certain virtue or merit, we are eager to have people know it any way we can and to have that virtue or merit ascribed to our imaginary existence. We diminish our true life in order to add something to our imaginary life, even to the point of willingly being cowards if it means acquiring the reputation of being brave, or losing our life with joy, as long as people talk about it.[10]

The tendency highlighted by Pascal has increased enormously in our current culture dominated by mass media, film, television and the world of entertainment in general. René Descartes said, "I think; therefore I am," but today that tends to be substituted with "I appear; therefore I am." At its origin the word *hypocrisy* was reserved for theater arts. It simply meant "to recite," to represent something on stage. Saint Augustine recalls this in his commentary on the beatitude of the pure in heart: "For hypocrites are pretenders, as it were setters forth of other characters, just as in the plays of the theatre."[11] Everything is playacting now on our television screens, even the news.

The origin of the word puts us on track to discover the nature of hypocrisy. It means making life a theater in which someone recites for an audience. It means putting on a mask, ceasing to be a person and becoming a character. Somewhere I read this description of the two states:

A fictive character is nothing more than the corruption of an authentic person. A person has a face; a character wears a mask. A person is drastically naked; a character is only clothing. A person loves authenticity and reality; a character lives a life of make-believe and artifice. A person follows his or her own convictions; a character follows a script. A person is humble and light; a character is cumbersome and unwieldy.

Theatrical fiction, however, is an innocent hypocrisy because it always maintains the distinction between the stage and real life. No one who attends a presentation of *Agamemnon* on stage (this is the example given by Augustine) thinks that the actor really is Agamemnon. The new and disquieting fact today is that there is a tendency to eliminate this distinction, transforming life itself into a show. This is the claim of the so-called "reality shows" that are flooding television networks throughout the world. According to the French philosopher Jean Baudrillard, it has become difficult now to distinguish between real events (9/11, the Gulf War) and their media presentation. Reality and virtual reality have merged.[12]

The call to interiority, which characterizes this beatitude and the whole Sermon on the Mount, is an invitation not to let ourselves be carried away by this tendency that empties a person, reducing him or her to an image or, even worse, to an insubstantial shadow. Søren Kierkegaard has drawn attention to the alienation that results from living a purely external life, always living before the eyes of other people and never simply in the sight of God and of one's own self or "I." A cattleman, he observes, can be an "I" before his herd—if he is living with them and has nothing else by which to measure himself. A king can be an "I" before his subjects and will feel himself to be an important "I." A baby is an "I" with regard to its parents, a citizen with regard to the state and so on. But each "I" here will be imperfect because it lacks an outside measure. "And what infinite reality...the self gains by being conscious of existing before God, by becoming a human self whose criterion is God!... [W]hat an infinite accent falls on the self by having God as the criterion."[13]

This sounds like a commentary on a saying from Saint Francis of Assisi: "For what a man is before God, that he is and nothing more."[14]

One Kind of Collective Hypocrisy

The social and cultural relevance of some beatitudes is often prominent. It is quite common to see "Blessed are the peacemakers" on banners in pacifist demonstrations, and the beatitude about the meek is rightly invoked to support the principle of nonviolence. However, the social relevance of the beatitude about the pure in heart is never spoken of, so this beatitude seems reserved exclusively for one's personal life. I am convinced, however, that this beatitude can exercise a much-needed critical function in our society today.

There are instances of individual hypocrisy but also instances of collective hypocrisy. I would like to highlight one form of collective hypocrisy in which we are very deeply immersed. Contrary to the ordinary meaning of the word, this hypocrisy does not consist in covering up but in uncovering, not in hiding but in showing. I am speaking of the exhibition of the human body, especially by women, passed off as art, as aesthetic pleasure and as overcoming taboos, while—unlike what happens in genuine art, for example, with Botticelli—it is really responding only to commercial interests and to audience demands.

This phenomenon is especially prominent in Italy. A while ago in a prestigious British newspaper, the *Financial Times*, a feature story was published entitled "Naked Ambition."[15] It was a denunciation of the Italian habit of exhibiting women's nude bodies in every possible way and for every possible reason. Adolescent Italian girls, it said, all want to be "showgirls." What happened to the feminist movement in Italy, we can ask, that in the past proposed to fight against the chauvinistic tendency to reduce women to their bodies and to sex?

Had it been the Italian bishops who denounced this, it would have probably fallen on deaf ears, but coming from a prestigious British newspaper, it was supported by a chorus of self-critical comments and a consensus of the major press organizations. The article addressing the problem in the *Corriere della Sera* (a major Italian newspaper) ended with this reflection:

> The whole world looks at us and laughs, and our media ignore the problem [so it had to be a foreign newspaper that told us about it]. Italy often criticizes the Arab and Muslim world, but when we consider the role of women in the media or in politics, people say, "Oh, but that's different."[16]

There are different analyses of this phenomenon. Everyone agrees in emphasizing that the chief responsibility belongs to the men who continue to exercise their power over women in this way, passing it off as aesthetic admiration. In another large daily Italian newspaper, *La Repubblica*, one woman lamented the fact that, instead of valuing her for her two degrees and the professional training she demonstrated, her colleagues basically valued her for quite other reasons.

Although this is all true, we also need to acknowledge a responsibility on the part of women. What men look at also depends on what women show of themselves (recently the belly button!). The word of God to Eve is again fulfilled: "Your desire shall be for your husband [the male], / and he shall rule over you" (Genesis 3:16). We are seeing the umpteenth form of domination and exploitation (unfortunately consensual) of women.

Now I will try to explain why I defined all this as a phenomenon of collective hypocrisy. People feign an innocence and nonchalance that is completely false. Everyone repeats, "What's the harm in it?" while they know very well that it is harmful and why it is harmful, so this is deceptive on their part. If hypocrisy means concealing true intentions behind false appearances, this is downright hypocrisy, whether on the part of men or of women.

It is hypocrisy for another reason as well. It reduces young women to "cover girls" or "showgirls"; it reduces them to their appearance, to being creatures without souls whose worth depends only on their value in the eyes of others. This kind of mentality, which is spreading among the youth, is deadly. It insinuates that to make one's fortune in life there is no need to apply oneself to study, to make the sacrifices required for good professional training, to study languages and so on. Young people are satisfied with capitalizing on their bodies, if they can, with a bit of dash and daring. Life, unfortunately, will see to it that the bill soon arrives: as soon as their bodies age and their youth fades, many young men and women will find themselves alone and unprepared to face life. These tragedies are daily occurrences.

One concrete way to counter this trend is to boycott the products or television programs that thrive on marketing of the female body. We can also communicate to the advertisers and the hosts of talk shows that we have had enough of this phenomenon that makes us look ridiculous in the eyes of the whole world, not to mention, of course, being reprehensible in the eyes of God. If people encourage the boycott of the industries that sell weapons or genetically engineered food, why not do as much for those who pollute the very sources of life? If we do not do this, then we, too, are responsible.

Religious Hypocrisy

The worst thing people can do is to use hypocrisy to judge others, whether society, the culture or the world. These are precisely the people to whom Jesus applies the category of hypocrites: "You hypocrite, first take the log out of your own eye, and then you will see clearly to take the speck out of your brother's eye" (Matthew 7:5).

As believers we should recall the saying of a Jewish rabbi in the time of Christ. According to him, 90 percent of the hypocrisy in the world at that time could be found in Jerusalem.[17] Hypocrisy especially seduces pious and religious people, and for one simple reason: Wherever an esteem for spiritual values and virtues (or for orthodoxy!) is strongest, the temptation is strongest to display those virtues so as not to be thought to lack them. Sometimes it is the very office we hold that moves us to do that. Saint Augustine writes:

> Since by reason of certain official positions in human society, it is necessary for us to be both loved and feared by men, the adversary of our true happiness keeps after us, and on every side amidst his snares he scatters the words, "Well done! Well done!" He does this so that, as we greedily gather up these words, we may be caught unawares, displace our joy from the truth, and place it among the deceits of men, and so that it may afford us pleasure to be feared and to be loved, not because of you but in place of you.[18]

The most pernicious hypocrisy is to conceal one's own hypocrisy. I do not remember, in any formulation for an examination of conscience, finding the questions, "Have I been a hypocrite? Have I been more concerned about people's opinion of me than about God's opinion?" At a certain point in life, I needed to introduce these questions into my examination of conscience for my own sake, and rarely have I been able to move on to the next question without being convicted.

One day the Gospel passage for the Mass was the parable of the talents. As I was listening to it, I suddenly understood something. Besides using one's talents and burying one's talents, there is a third possibility: using one's talents, yes, but for oneself, for one's own glory and advantage, and not for the master. That is perhaps a more serious sin than burying talents. That day, at Communion time, I had to do what some thieves do who are caught in the act and who, full of shame, empty out their pockets and lay what they have stolen at the feet of the owner.

Jesus has left us a simple and superb way to rectify our intentions several times during the day, namely, the first three requests in the *Our Father*: "Hallowed be thy name. / Thy kingdom come. / Thy will be done" (Matthew 6:9–10). These phrases can be recited as prayers but also as declarations of our intentions: Everything that I do, I want to do so that it sanctifies your name, so that it makes your kingdom come, so that your will is done.

It would be an invaluable contribution to society and to the Christian community if the beatitude about the pure in heart helped keep alive in us a longing for a clean, sincere world without hypocrisy—collective or individual, religious or lay— a world in which actions correspond to words, words to thoughts and one's thoughts to God's thoughts.

This will not happen fully until we see the heavenly Jerusalem, the city clear as crystal (see Revelation 21:10–11), but we should at least aim for it. A fairy tale called *Il paese di vetro* [The Country of Glass] is about a character who magically ends up in a country made of glass: glass houses, glass birds, glass trees and people who move like graceful statuettes of glass. Nothing has ever been broken in this country, because all have learned how to move gently so as not to harm anything. When people meet each other, they respond to questions before they are formulated, because even thoughts are open and transparent. No one tries to lie, knowing that everyone can read everyone else's mind.[19]

We can shudder just thinking about what would happen if this were the case now in our relationships. But it is helpful to propose this openness to ourselves at least as an ideal. It is the path that leads to the beatitude "Blessed are the pure in heart, for they shall see God."

Chapter Seven

BLESSED ARE THE PEACEMAKERS, FOR THEY SHALL BE CALLED SONS OF GOD

Who Are the Peacemakers?

The seventh beatitude says, "Blessed are the peacemakers, for they shall be called sons of God" (Matthew 5:9). Rather than speaking about our need *to be* something (poor, mournful, meek, pure of heart), this beatitude, like the beatitude about the merciful, speaks about our need *to do* something.

The word *eirinopoioi* means "those who work for peace, who make peace." The sense is not so much that they reconcile with their own enemies but that they help enemies to reconcile. "These are people who love peace so much that they are not afraid of compromising their own peace by intervening in conflicts to procure peace among those who are in dissension."[1]

Peacemakers, then, is not synonymous with "peaceful people," that is, calm and tranquil people who avoid conflict as much as possible. (These people are proclaimed blessed in the beatitude about the meek.) Neither is it a synonym for *pacifists*, if by pacifists we mean those who side against war (most often against one of the contenders in the war!) without doing anything to reconcile the warring factions with each other. The most accurate synonym might be *peace brokers*.

In New Testament times kings, and the Roman emperor in particular, were called peace brokers. Augustus listed at the top of his accomplishments establishing peace in the world through his military victories (*parta victoriis pax*), and he had the famous *Ara Pacis* (the Altar to Peace) built in Rome.

Some have thought that the gospel beatitude is meant to counter this interpretation and offer a different explanation of who the real peacemakers are and how peace gets promoted: through victories, yes, but victories over oneself, not over one's enemies, not by destroying the enemy but by destroying hostility itself, as Jesus did on the cross (see Ephesians 2:16). However, the prevailing opinion today is that an understanding of this beatitude must take into account the Bible and Jewish sources that view helping people in conflict to reconcile and live in peace as one of the chief works of mercy. On Christ's lips the beatitude about peacemakers derives from the new commandment of brotherly love and is one way in which the love of neighbor is expressed.

It is surprising, then, to hear from the same lips of Christ an assertion that seems contradictory: "Do you think that I have come to give peace on earth? No, I tell you, but rather division" (Luke 12:51). Matthew, instead of the word *division*, uses "a sword" (Matthew 10:34). However, there is no real contradiction here.

The issue is understanding what kind of peace and unity

Jesus came to bring and what kind of peace and unity he came to remove. He came to bring peace and unity to whatever is good and leads to eternal life, and he came to remove the false peace and unity that only lulls the conscience to sleep and leads to ruin.

Jesus did not come with the intention of bringing division and war. Nevertheless, his coming inevitably results in division and conflict, because he brings people to a decision point, and we know that, in the face of a decision, human free will responds in different and varied ways. His words and his person make what people hide in their hearts rise to the surface. The elderly Simeon predicted that when he took the baby Jesus in his arms: "This child is set for the fall and rising of many in Israel, / and for a sign that is spoken against, / ... / that thoughts out of many hearts may be revealed" (Luke 2:34–35).

The first victim of this contradiction, the first to suffer from the "sword" that he came to bring on earth, will be himself, so that in this conflict he will bring life back to us.

The Message for World Day of Peace
One could say that the beatitude about the peacemakers is the one par excellence for the church of Rome and its bishop. One of the most valuable services to Christianity by the papacy, in its best moments, has been to promote peace among the different churches and, in certain eras, among Christian leaders as well. The first apostolic letter by a pope, by Saint Clement I, dating from around AD 96 (perhaps even

before the fourth Gospel), was written to bring peace to the church in Corinth, which was torn apart by dissension.

The history of the church is full of episodes in which local churches, bishops or abbots quarrelling with one another or with their flock turned to the pope as the arbiter of peace. I am certain that this is still one of the most frequent services rendered to the universal church, even if it is one of the less well known. Vatican diplomacy and apostolic nuncios have as one of their goals being instruments in the service of peace. It is a service that cannot happen without some kind of real jurisdictional power. To be aware of its enormous value, we only need to see the difficulties that surface where it is absent.

For some time now the pope's service on behalf of peace is also expressed through his message for World Peace Day, which he delivers at the beginning of each new year. I would like to discuss Pope Benedict XVI's message for 2007 as we enter into reflection on this beatitude.[2] It deals with peace in every area, from the personal sphere to the larger spheres of politics, economics, ecology and international organizations. Although these spheres are different, they are unified in having the human being as their primary object, as reflected in the title of the pope's address, "The Human Person, the Heart of Peace."

There is a central affirmation in the message that is the key to understanding the whole of it. The pope says:

[P]eace is both gift and task. If it is true that peace between individuals and peoples—the ability to live together and to build relationships of justice and solidarity—calls for unfailing commitment on our part, it is also true, and indeed more so, that *peace is a gift from God*. Peace is an aspect of God's activity, made manifest both in the creation of an orderly and harmonious universe and also in the redemption of humanity that needs to be rescued from the disorder of sin. Creation and Redemption thus provide a key that helps us begin to understand the meaning of our life on earth.[3]

These words help us understand the beatitude about the peacemakers, which in turn sheds a remarkable light on these words. Let us meditate on peace as a gift and a task.

Peace as a Gift

God himself, and not any particular human being, is the true and supreme peacemaker. Precisely because of this, those who work for peace are called the "sons of God," since they resemble him, they imitate him, they do what he does. The papal message says that peace is a characteristic of the divine action in creation and redemption, whether it be action on God's part or on Christ's part.

Scripture refers to "the peace of God" (Philippians 4:7) and even more often to "the God of peace" (Romans 15:33). Peace indicates not only something that God *does* or *gives* but also what God *is*. Peace is that which reigns in God.

Almost all the other religions during biblical times present divine worlds that are internally in conflict. The Babylonian and Greek cosmogonies speak of divinities that are warring among themselves. In the Gnostic Christian heresy, there is no unity and peace among the heavenly aeons, and the existence of the physical world is merely the result of an accident and of disharmony occurring in the upper world. Against this religious backdrop one can better understand the novelty and absolute distinctiveness of the doctrine of the Trinity as a perfect unity of love within a plurality of persons.

In one of its hymns the church calls the Trinity "an ocean of peace," and this is not just a poetic phrase. What strikes one the most in contemplating the icon of the Trinity by Andrei Rublëv is the sense of superhuman peace that emanates from it. The artist succeeded in transferring into an image the motto of Saint Sergius of Radonezh, for whose monastery the icon was painted: "Contemplating the Trinity, to overcome the hateful divisions of this world."[4]

The one who has best extolled the divine peace that comes from beyond history is Pseudo-Dionysius the Aeropagite. Peace, for him, is one of the names of God, in the same way that Love is a divine name.[5] In addition, it is said of Christ that he himself "is our peace" (Ephesians 2:14). When he says, "My peace I give to you" (John 14:27), he is transmitting that which he is.

There is an unbreakable link between peace as a gift from above and the Holy Spirit. It is not insignificant that they are both represented by the symbol of a dove. On Easter night Jesus gave his disciples, almost in the same breath, peace and the Holy Spirit: "Peace be with you" (John 20:21). Having said this, he breathed on them and said, "Receive the Holy

Spirit" (John 20:22). Peace, says Paul, is a "fruit of the Spirit" (Galatians 5:22).

But what exactly is this peace that we are talking about? The definition given by Saint Augustine has become classic: "Peace... is the calm that comes of order."[6] Basing his thought on that, Saint Thomas says that there are three kinds of order: with oneself, with God and with others. Consequently there are three types of peace: interior peace, wherein a person is at peace with himself or herself; peace with God, wherein a person submits himself or herself completely to God's will; and the peace related to one's neighbor, wherein a person lives at peace with everyone.[7]

In the Bible, however, *shalom*, peace, means more than simple tranquility due to order. It also indicates well-being, rest, safety, success, glory. At times it even means the totality of messianic blessings and is a synonym for salvation and for the good:

> How beautiful upon the mountains
>   are the feet of him who brings good tidings,
> who publishes *peace*, who brings good tidings of *good*,
>   who publishes *salvation*. (Isaiah 52:7, emphasis added)

The new covenant is called "a covenant of peace" (Ezekiel 37:26), and the gospel is called the "gospel of peace" (Ephesians 6:15); it is as though the word *peace* summarizes the whole content of the covenant and of the gospel.

In the Old Testament peace is often set alongside righteousness: "Righteousness and peace will kiss each other"

(Psalm 85:10). In the New Testament it is often set alongside grace. When Paul writes, "Since we are justified by faith, we have peace with God" (Romans 5:1), it is clear that "peace with God" carries the same pregnant meaning that is implied in "the grace of God."

Peace as a Task: Religious Peace

The pope's message says that peace, besides being a gift, is also a task. Peace as a task is primarily what the beatitude about the peacemakers is addressing. If God, and historically the Risen Christ, is the true source of Christian peace, then being a peacemaker does not mean inventing or creating peace but transmitting it, passing on the peace of God and the peace of Christ, "which passes all understanding" (Philippians 4:7). "Grace to you and peace *from God* our Father and *the Lord Jesus Christ*" (Romans 1:7, emphasis added): This is the peace that the apostle is transmitting to the Christians in Rome. We cannot be the source, but we can be channels of that peace. The prayer attributed to Saint Francis of Assisi expresses it perfectly: "Lord, make me an instrument of your peace."

The condition for being instruments of peace is to remain united to its source, which is the will of God. "In His will is our peace," says one of Dante's souls in Paradise.[8] The secret of interior peace is a total and continually renewed abandonment to the will of God. To preserve or reclaim this peace in one's heart, it helps to repeat often with Saint Teresa of Avila:

Let nothing disturb thee;

Let nothing dismay thee:
All things pass;
God never changes.
Patience attains
All that it strives for.
He who has God
Finds he lacks nothing:
God alone suffices.[9]

The apostolic *parenesis*, or instruction, is full of practical pointers about what promotes or hinders peace. One of the most well-known passages is in the Letter of James:

For where jealousy and selfish ambition exist, there will be disorder and every vile practice. But the wisdom from above is first pure, then peaceable, gentle, open to reason, full of mercy and good fruits, without uncertainty or insincerity. And the harvest of righteousness is sown in peace by those who make peace. (James 3:16–18)

Every effort to make peace needs to begin from this very personal sphere. Peace is like the wake left by a great ship, which spreads out to infinity but begins from one point, and the point in this case is the human heart. The message of John Paul II for World Peace Day in 1984 had as its title "From a New Heart, Peace Is Born."

But I do not want to linger on the personal sphere. Today a new area of difficult and urgent work is opening up for peacemakers: promoting peace among religions and with religion, that is, peace among religions themselves and peace between believers from various religions and the secular unbelieving world. The theologian Hans Küng introduced the following slogan during the international meeting of the Parliament of the World's Religions in Chicago in 1993:

> For there can be:
>
> No peace among the nations without peace among the religions.
>
> No peace among the religions without dialogue between the religions.[10]

The rationale for a serious dialogue among religions—based not only on timely reasons of which we are well aware but also on a solid theological foundation—is that "in our diversity, we find ourselves before faith in the one God," as Benedict XVI said during his visit to the Blue Mosque of Istanbul.[11] This is the truth with which Saint Paul began his discourse to the Areopagus in Athens (see Acts 17:28).

Subjectively we have different ideas about God. For us Christians, God is the "Father of our Lord Jesus Christ" who is not fully known except through him (see Ephesians 1:3–14). *Objectively*, however, we know well that there can only be one God. There is "one God and Father of us all, who is above all and through all and in all" (Ephesians 4:6). Every nation and language has its own word for the sun, but there is only one sun!

Another theological foundation for this dialogue is our faith in the Holy Spirit. As the Spirit of redemption and the Spirit of grace, he is the bond of peace among the baptized

Christians of various faiths, but as the Spirit of creation, *Spiritus creator*, he is the bond of peace among believers in all religions and even among all human beings of good will. "Every truth by whomsoever spoken," Saint Thomas wrote, "is from the Holy Ghost."[12]

However, just as this creator Spirit guided the Old Testament prophets toward Christ (see 1 Peter 1:11), so, too, we Christians believe that, in a way known only to God, he guides people to Christ and his paschal mystery in his action outside the church. Just as the Son does nothing without the Father (see John 5:19), the Holy Spirit does nothing without the Son.

Peace Without Religion?

The secularized West, to tell the truth, hopes for a different kind of religious peace, one that results from the disappearance of all religion. John Lennon, one of the great idols of modern rock music, wrote the immensely popular "Imagine," with a pleasing melody and lyrics that encourage us to dream of a world that has no heaven, no hell, no religion, no country, "nothing to kill or die for." Few people realize the song's nature is anything but pacifist. According to Lennon it is an "anti-religious, anti-nationalistic, anti-conventional, anti-capitalistic song, but because it's sugar-coated, it's accepted."[13]

Is a world in which there is no longer religion, country or private property really desirable? Wasn't this exactly what the totalitarian regimes wanted to achieve (and we know with

what result)? Everyone would be happy if there were nothing
to kill for in the world anymore, but what would we say about
a world in which there is nothing to die for?

If such a dream should be achieved, it would really be a
world that is more impoverished and more squalid than can
possibly be imagined—a neutralized world in which all dif-
ferences are abolished and in which people are destined to
tear each other apart rather than to live in peace. This is
because, as René Girard has explained, when everyone wants
the same things, the "mimetic desire" gets out of control, and
with that comes rivalry and war.[14]

Someone else had already proposed, "No more Heaven, no
more Hell; nothing but earth."[15] Perhaps it was from this
author that Lennon got his idea. But then this is the same
author who stated that "Hell is—other people!"[16] The hell that
was "below us" has shifted to be "among us" now.

The pope's message dedicates a paragraph to the difficulty
that we meet today in the relationship between religion and
the secular world:

> As far as *the free expression of personal faith* is concerned,
> another disturbing symptom of lack of peace in the world
> is represented by the difficulties that both Christians
> and the followers of other religions frequently encounter
> in publicly and freely professing their religious convic-
> tions. There are regimes that impose a single religion
> upon everyone, while secular regimes often lead not so
> much to violent persecution as to systematic cultural

denigration of religious beliefs. In both instances, a fundamental human right is not being respected, with serious repercussions for peaceful coexistence.[17]

There is a sign of this attempt to marginalize religious beliefs every December, namely, the campaign in America and various countries of Europe against the religious symbols of Christmas. The reason cited is the desire not to offend people of other religions who live among us, especially Muslims. But this is only a pretext. It is actually part of secularized society—not the Muslims—who do not want these symbols. Muslims have nothing against Christian Christmas, which they also honor. In the Koran there is a sura dedicated to the birth of Jesus that is worth knowing about and that could encourage dialogue and friendship among religions:

Behold! The angel said:
"O Mary! Allah giveth thee
Glad tidings of a Word
From Him: his name
Will be Christ Jesus.
The son of Mary, held in honour
In this world and the Hereafter
And of (the company of) those
Nearest to Allah.
. . . .
She said: "O my Lord!
How shall I have a son
When no man hath touched me?"

He said: "Even so:
Allah createth
What He willeth:
When He hath decreed
A Plan, He but saith
To it, 'Be,' and it is!"[18]

We have reached the height of absurdity when some Muslims celebrate the birth of Christ and tell us that "it is not Muslims who do not believe in the miraculous birth of Christ,"[19] while people who call themselves Christians want to make Christmas a winter festival populated only by reindeer and teddy bears.

We Christians cannot, however, let ourselves become resentful and argumentative with the secular world. Alongside the dialogue and the peace among religions, there is another task for the peacemaker: peace between believers and nonbelievers, between religious people and the secular world that is dismissive or hostile to religion. We need to give a reason, with firmness, for the hope that is in us but to do so, as the First Letter of Peter exhorts, "with gentleness and reverence" (1 Peter 3:15–16).

Reverence in this case does not mean a human respect that keeps Jesus hidden to avoid arousing reactions. It means a respect for the interior life that is known only to God and that no one can violate or force to change. It does not mean putting Jesus aside but demonstrating Jesus and the gospel by our lives. We only hope that equal respect will be shown by others toward Christians, which unfortunately has often been lacking up until now.

On Christmas Eve we hear the words of the angelic proclamation, "On earth peace among men with whom he is pleased" (Luke 2:14). This does not mean, "Let there *be* peace," but, "There *is* peace." This is not a wish but an announcement of fact. "The birth of the Lord," Saint Leo the Great said, "is the birth of peace."[20]

How can we respond to the infinite gift that the Father gives the world in giving us his only-begotten Son? If there is an error to avoid at Christmas, it is to recycle a gift and offer it, by mistake, to the very person from whom we received it. Well, with God we cannot help but make this mistake all the time! The only possible thanksgiving is to offer him Jesus, who is his Son but also our brother. The unique gift that is worthy of God is the Eucharist.

And what gift shall we give Jesus? One text in the Eastern liturgy at Christmas says, "What shall we offer you, Christ, for becoming man on earth? All creatures made by you offer you their thanks: the angels offer their songs; the heavens a star; the earth a cave; the wilderness a manger; and we offer you a virgin mother."[21]

BLESSED ARE THOSE WHO ARE PERSECUTED FOR RIGHTEOUSNESS' SAKE, FOR THEIRS IS THE KINGDOM OF HEAVEN

Two Reasons for Persecution: Righteousness and the Name of Christ

The beatitude about the persecuted is one of the few (four in all) that are attested by both Matthew and Luke, and it is the only one that is followed by a brief comment by Jesus. A look at the parallel texts of Matthew and Luke at the beginning of the book will help us better understand the reflections that follow.

The issue that best distinguishes and characterizes the two versions is the reason for which there is persecution: "on account of the Son of man" in Luke (6:22) and "for righteousness' sake" in Matthew (5:10). In Luke's case it is a Christological reason: The disciples who suffer for their faith in Christ are proclaimed blessed. This has a historical basis: It has in mind the concrete situation of the church as the object of discrimination and hostility by the surrounding society, especially Jewish society at the beginning.

In Matthew's case the reason for persecution is moral, and it has a universal basis. The addressees of the beatitude are not a narrowly defined group; the group includes all those who are persecuted in any way for righteousness. There is an underlying Christological reason in Matthew as well—righteousness for the sake of Christ—but it takes on a wider significance. The righteousness he speaks of is of course the righteousness of the gospel, the righteousness of the kingdom ("seek first his kingdom and his righteousness" [Matthew 6:33]), which is expressed through the works of righteousness (see Matthew 25:31–46). However, precisely for this reason it is a broader and more inclusive category than the category of those persecuted because of the historical person of Christ.

We can notice a certain evolution in the way this beatitude has been interpreted over the centuries. In antiquity and, in part, during the Middle Ages, Luke's Christological reason for persecution prevailed. Martyrs were only those who were persecuted for faith in Christ. However, in modern times, especially in our day, the moral and broader reason—"for righteousness' sake"—has assumed a new importance. Martyrs are considered (even by the official church) to be not only those who are actually put to death for their faith in Christ but also those who lay down their lives out of love for their neighbor, like Saint Maximilian Mary Kolbe; those who die to defend the rights of the oppressed, like Oscar Romero; those who die to defend their chastity, like Saint Maria Goretti. Faith in Christ is the essential requirement for every authentic Christian martyrdom, but faith is not always or necessarily its immediate cause.

Two Forms of Persecution: Death and Marginalization
The persecution of Christ's disciples can assume two different forms that are important to recognize today. They are described in a paradigmatic and prophetic way in chapter thirteen of Revelation through the images of the two beasts: the beast rising out of the sea (Revelation 13:1–10) and the beast rising out of the earth (Revelation 13:11–18). The beast rising out of the sea is identified with a political power that sets itself up in place of God and "make[s] war on the saints...to conquer them" (see Revelation 13:7), condemning some to prison and some to the sword. The second beast, which rises from the earth, also persecutes the saints but in a different way.

In general the second beast does not put Christians to death but marginalizes or ostracizes them. Its task is to make "the earth and its inhabitants worship the first beast" (Revelation 13:12). It has the power of occult persuasion, a kind of ministry of propaganda for the Dragon. It forces people to adore the first beast and to be dominated by it, initiating for that goal the horrible practice of being "marked on the right hand or the forehead" (Revelation 13:16). Without the mark it is impossible to "buy or sell" (Revelation 13:17) and therefore impossible to be part of society (a sad precedent of the Star of David imposed on the Jews by the Nazis). The second beast prefers to rely not on arms but on culture and public opinion.

The description in Revelation has an obvious *historical dimension.* The first beast has almost unanimously been identified as the Roman Empire and its representatives, in particular Domitian, who made the divine cult of the emperor official, and Nero, the instigator of the first official persecution of Christians. The second beast represents the religious and cultural propaganda apparatus that promoted the imperial ideology, especially in Asia Minor.

However, the description also has an obvious *prophetic dimension*: It outlines the picture of the situation for the disciples of the Lamb in every era of history. It is a mistake to try to find in the descriptions in Revelation—in particular those of the two beasts—precise correlations with events and facts in history, as has so often been done, leading to aberrant conclusions. It would be equally foolish, however, not to make use of this prophetic denunciation to shed light on subsequent situations in the church and in the world.

This issue is especially evident in our day. The atheistic totalitarian regimes and military dictatorships that incarnated the first beast and made so many martyrs in the preceding century have fallen, and it is the second beast that holds sway at present. Pope Benedict XVI seems to apply the paradigm of the two beasts to present circumstances when, in the message for World Peace Day in 2007 already referred to, he writes, "There are regimes that impose a single religion upon everyone, while secular regimes often lead not so much to violent persecution as to systematic cultural denigration of religious beliefs."[1]

Cruel persecutions are not over by any means. Almost every day we receive news of Christians being put to death or forced into exile by extremist fringes in Islamic countries. It is an odd thing that a journalist of Muslim faith, Magdi Allam, is the one who launched the movement in Italy called "Save the Christians" in order to rouse public opinion, which has been so strangely apathetic to this problem.[2]

In our secularized Western world, persecution usually takes the second form, which uses opinion instead of the sword. The exegete Heinrich Schlier has made a penetrating analysis of this fact, commenting on the verse from Scripture that speaks of "the prince of the power of the air" (Ephesians 2:2). He draws attention to its role, in this regard, in shaping public opinion. The "spirit of the world," as Paul calls it (1 Corinthians 2:12), or the spirit of the age, creates a spiritual atmosphere in which demonic powers act behind the scenes. This spirit of the world is

> so intense and powerful that no individual can escape it. It serves as a norm and is taken for granted. To act, think or speak against this spirit is regarded as non-sensical or even as wrong and criminal. It is "in" this spirit that men encounter the world and affairs, which means that they accept the world as this spirit presents it to them.... [The prince of this world, hidden in the spiritual atmosphere during different time periods,] gives everything natural or human.... an appearance of [his] own making.[3]

Scripture's qualifying label for this power, "of the air," is particularly pertinent today, since this ideology uses the means of mass media as its preferred vehicle. We indeed have messages transmitted through the air: radio, television, Internet and so on.

What is the difference between these two forms of persecution? State atheism fights openly against faith, while secularism tends to make faith appear irrelevant or even as residue from earlier stages that human consciousness has surpassed. "Religious faith is, precisely *because* we are still-evolving creatures, ineradicable," says one secular writer. "It will never die out, or at least not until we get over our fear of death, and of the dark, and of the unknown, and of each other."[4]

According to this prediction, religion will survive this current attack as well, as it has survived an infinite number of other attacks that have preceded it. People attempt to explain this embarrassing fact by making religion just a temporary byproduct that is due to humanity's present condition of "still evolving." In this way the atheist intellectual tacitly assumes the role of being the only one who has risen above this situation by anticipating the goal of evolution and who, like Nietzsche's Zarathustra, returns to earth to enlighten mere mortals about reality.

The Characteristics of a True Martyr: Love, Humility and Grace
Not everyone who is persecuted belongs to the category of those whom Jesus proclaims blessed. The fundamental stipulation is that there is no mixture whatsoever between the

roles of the persecuted and the persecutor.

One terrible case of that shift in roles between persecuted and persecutors, for example, was the attitude of Christians toward Jews through the course of the centuries. The Jews were also hated by others, exiled, insulted and rejected "for the sake of the Son of man," but in a very different sense than the one intended and approved by Christ.

When this distinction between the two roles disappears or is blurred, we then have the aberrant cases of suicide-martyrs or murder-martyrs. The persecuted, or those who think themselves so, become transformed into persecutors, the executioner-martyrs. It is not up to us Christians to judge the concept of martyrdom at play in other religions, but we need to be clear about who the Gospel says the truly persecuted are. Jesus advised his disciples to be like "sheep in the midst of wolves" (Matthew 10:16). He told them, "When they persecute you in one town, flee to the next" (Matthew 10:23). This saying is the basis for the Fathers' rejection of every attitude of violent resistance, even defending flight in the face of persecution if circumstances require it.[5]

Another kind of blurring between these roles is martyrdom-provocation, in which the martyr is the one who causes the persecution because of a defiant attitude. Today we would not find, for example, the actions of the first Franciscan martyrs acceptable: Disembarking in Morocco, they began to preach faith in the open square, publicly calling for the Saracens throughout the city, leaders and people, to abandon their faith and convert to Christianity.[6]

Saint Francis was already sensitive to this point because, even though he eulogized these martyrs as "true minor friars" for their courage and good faith, he proposed a way of approaching "the Saracens and other nonbelievers" other than openly proclaiming the Christian faith and exhorting them to conversion as soon as possible. This second approach, as he explains in "The Earlier Rule," was "not to engage in arguments or disputes, but to be subject *to every human creature for God's sake* (1 Peter 2:13) and to acknowledge that they [themselves] are Christians."[7]

Concerned about the polemic with the Donatists, who justified suicide-martyrdom, Saint Augustine reflected for a long time on the true nature of Christian martyrdom, deciding in the end that "men are made martyrs not by the amount of their suffering, but by the cause [for] which they suffer."[8] By itself, even this saying could lead to an erroneous interpretation. So many have died for a cause that was mistaken—and even evil—believing it to be good. This is why Augustine feels the need to qualify and to amplify this definition. It is also not enough to die for Christ, for faith, if one does so without love, with antagonism against someone. Let us remember Paul's saying: "If I give away all I have, and if I deliver my body to be burned, but have not love, I gain nothing" (1 Corinthians 13:3).

Augustine proposes love as a criterion for recognizing a true martyr and also proposes, in the case of the schismatic Donatists in particular, a criterion of love for the unity of the church. It is with love and forgiveness that Christ, Stephen and many others after them died, and that is the identifying sign of an authentic Christian martyr. Augustine's idea that "the cause makes the martyr" is enhanced by his other idea that "loves makes the martyr."[9]

It is moving to find so many centuries later, in that same northern Africa where Augustine worked, one of the most shining testimonies of martyrdom accompanied by love. I am referring to the seven Trappist monks slaughtered in May 1996 in Tibhirine, Algeria, by a group of fundamentalist Muslims. A few days earlier, when a tragic ending grew increasingly likely, the prior, Dom Christian de Chergé, wrote a spiritual testament that will remain one of the most sublime expressions of the Christian spirituality of martyrdom: "I should like, when the time comes, to have a moment of spiritual clarity which would allow me to beg forgiveness of God and of my fellow human beings, and at the same time to forgive with all my heart the one who will strike me down."[10]

The prior did not want his possible death and those of his fellow monks to be blamed on all of Islam or on the Algerian people. Neither did he want the blame to fall on the actual executioner, "especially if he says he is acting in fidelity to what he believes to be Islam."[11] He concludes, directly addressing the one that perhaps one day will stand before him with a sword, "And also you, my last minute friend, who will not have known what you were doing: Yes, I want this THANK YOU and this 'A-DIEU' to be for you, too, because in God's face I see yours. May we meet again as happy thieves in Paradise, if it please God, the Father of us both. Amen!"[12]

A comparison that Augustine develops in *De Civitate Dei* (*The City of God*) leads him to highlight a second essential quality of Christian martyrdom, humility. He is dealing with a pagan culture that exalts those who became martyrs and suicides for the sake of honor: Lucretia, Cato, Mucius Scaevola, Marcus Attilius Regulus. According to Augustine, these pagans demonstrated strong resolve but not true greatness of soul. True greatness would have led them to endure their misfortune or humiliation with fortitude, rather than escaping by taking their own lives.

The humility of martyrs is also shown by their fear and revulsion in the face of death: "They are martyrs, yes; but they were human beings."[13] We are very far from the spirit of the wise stoic who is certain that even if the whole world collapses around him, he will remain undaunted among its ruins.[14] The Christian martyr will never face this trial relying on his or her own strength but only on the grace of God. In the debate with the Pelagians, Augustine's affirmation that "the cause makes the martyr" is enhanced by yet another truth, "Grace makes the martyr."

In light of Augustine's amplified definition of a martyr, certain points of resemblance between the attitudes of the martyr and those of the pagan hero in so much pagan martyrology seem ingenuous and anachronistic. If the statement attributed to Saint Lawrence on being martyred on a burning grate—"This part is cooked, so turn me over and eat"[15]—were historical (it is not), it would make him more like Gaius Mucius Scaevola[16] than like Jesus Christ.

The way preparation for martyrdom is presented in Georges Bernanos's play *Dialogues of the Carmelites*[17] appears profoundly Augustinian and Christian, as does martyrdom in the narrative that is the basis for the play, Gertrud von le Fort's *The Song at the Scaffold*[18] (the story of the sixteen Carmelite nuns of Compiègne martyred during the French Revolution). The young nun Blanche of the Agony of Christ becomes terrified at the prospect of martyrdom and flees, separating herself from the other sisters. At the last minute, however, she finds the strength to come forth on her own and to climb up to the guillotine singing the last stanza of *Veni Creator*. This follows the pattern of Jesus, who agonizes when facing his imminent passion and exclaims to his disciples, "The spirit indeed is willing, but the flesh is weak" (Matthew 26:41), but then says resolutely, "Rise, let us be going" (Matthew 26:46).

The play *Murder in the Cathedral*, by T.S. Eliot, also splendidly reflects Christian martyrdom. For him the last temptation that a martyr has to face is pride. This is the implication of what the Fourth Tempter tells Thomas à Becket:

What can compare with the glory of Saints
Dwelling forever in the presence of God ?
What earthly glory, of king or emperor[?]

. . .

Seek the way of martyrdom, make yourself the lowest
On earth, to be high in heaven.[19]

The archbishop addresses his last words to his people before the assassins sent by the king reach him: "A Christian martyrdom [is not] the effect of a man's will to become a Saint.... A martyrdom is always the design of God, for His love of men.... [T]he true martyr...no longer desires anything for himself, not even the glory of being a martyr."[20] Martyrdom is a grace.

Persecuted Unjustly or Justly?

In his very comprehensive commentary on the beatitudes, the exegete Jacques Dupont highlights a particular point in Matthew's version: "Blessed are you when men revile you and persecute you and *utter* all kinds of evil against you *falsely* on my account" (Matthew 5:11, emphasis added). According to him the words "utter falsely" (*pseudomenoi*) reflect the Gospel writer's concern to distinguish unjust persecution from just persecution.[21]

The Gospel writer, perhaps spurred by his ecclesial experiences, points to the possibility that Christians might be accused not wrongly but rightly, not falsely but accurately. His is not an isolated voice in the apostolic church. Saint Peter has already made a distinction between suffering for being a Christian and suffering for being "a murderer, or a thief, or a wrongdoer" (1 Peter 4:15), and Saint Paul often exhorts believers to conduct themselves in such a way as not to give pagans a reason to blaspheme (see Romans 2:17–24, for example).

The first Christian preachers also present the possibility that persecution could be caused by the dishonorable conduct of Christians and not simply because of hatred for

Christ. An anonymous second-century author wrote, "For when the Gentiles hear from our mouth the oracles of God, they wonder at their beauty and grandeur; afterwards, when they find out that their [Christians'] works are unworthy of the words they speak, they turn from this to blasphemy."[22]

Never so much as in this case do the beatitudes appear to us as the self-portrait of Jesus, the one in whom they are fully and exemplarily fulfilled. "There is only one," wrote the philosopher Søren Kierkegaard, "who was truly persecuted and unjustly: Jesus Christ." When we are persecuted and suffer, he says, we should join the good thief on the cross in saying, "We indeed [suffer] justly; for we are receiving the due reward of our deeds; but this man has done nothing wrong" (Luke 23:41). Even if we are not guilty of committing a particular wrong that is imputed to us, we are never completely exempt from guilt. Only God, when he suffers, suffers in absolute innocence.[23]

Perhaps the only exception is the suffering of innocent children, and this is precisely the reason it is so hard for us to accept. Their suffering joins the suffering of the Lamb without sin, and it is only this perspective that can keep a believer from despair about it.

All of this should help believers not to fall into pointless persecution complexes in the face of growing hostility toward them in the secular world. Such hostility is never without some reason. Even today, as in the time of the anonymous author of the "Second Letter of Clement," many people admire the goodness of Christ and the truths of the gospel but are scandalized by the conduct of those who profess to be Christians.

The ideal attitude for the Christian facing opposition in the world is outlined by Saint Paul: "When reviled, we bless; when persecuted, we endure; when slandered, we try to conciliate" (1 Corinthians 4:12–13). The author of the Epistle to Diognetus saw this approach in the Christians of his time: "They love all men, but are persecuted by all.... They are reviled, and they bless."[24]

The beatitude about those who are persecuted for righteousness, though, is not lived out only on exceptional occasions or in the clash between the church and the world, but also in daily events, in the conflicts and opposition that life brings to everyone. Jesus warns that "righteousness," that is, duty and conscience, often leads us to say and do things that can arouse opposition against us, even in the narrow circle of our families: "Three against two and two against three; they will be divided, father against son and son against father, mother against daughter and daughter against her mother, mother-in-law against her daughter-in-law and daughter-in-law against her mother-in-law" (Luke 12:52–53). This also happens within the church.

Before Descending the Mount

Having reached the end of our reflections on the beatitudes, I would like to pause for a moment to take a look at all of them together.

A while ago the community of Brescia organized a series of

public conferences on the beatitudes, asking people in education, finance and politics to comment on them. I was assigned the beatitude about the pure in heart, and the writer Erri De Luca was assigned the beatitude about the poor in spirit. He gave an assessment of the beatitudes that I find very accurate:

> The system of values has been turned upside down. A series of new joys is contrasted to the paltry scale of earthly values. The happy people are now the mild, those who hunger, those who thirst for righteousness, and the merciful. The innovation is shocking. These joys burn like a firebrand in one's hands.... Never have official categories and rankings been so reversed, and not by an insurrection but at the urging of a joy unknown to the powerful.... Their innovation has not yet found a place in the earth.[25]

There is perhaps something to clarify about his last statement. Jesus said, "The kingdom of God is not coming with signs to be observed; nor will they say, 'Behold, here it is!' or 'There!' for behold, the kingdom of God is in your midst" (Luke 17:20–21). This is particularly true for the beatitudes. They are operative already, at least in part, in this world, but not in the way that the world would expect. No one can count the human hearts that have already experienced in this life the happiness promised by Christ to the poor, the meek, the pure in heart.

Saint Thomas Aquinas notes that up to this point the mournful are comforted by "the Holy Spirit, Who is called the *Paraclete*, i.e., the Comforter"; those who hunger are satisfied with the Bread of Life; the merciful obtain mercy; those who purify themselves of evil see God in some way; and those who overcome impulses to anger are called the children of God.[26] But this does not clarify everything. This fulfillment for a few leaves unsatisfied those who grieve for the poverty, hunger and injustice experienced by entire groups of people.

In that sense we can understand the exclamation of my friend De Luca, "Their innovation has not yet found a place in the earth." One could exclaim about the beatitudes what Charles Péguy's Joan of Arc says about the Our Father: "Our father,...how far is your kingdom from coming.... Our father,... how far is your will from being done."[27] How far the hungry are, O God, from being satisfied, the mournful from being comforted and the meek from inheriting the earth!

The solution is elsewhere. To understand the beatitudes we need to start with the *apodosis*, that is, with the promise tied to each of them. The promises are almost always in the future and point to another life: blessed are those who mourn because they "shall be comforted"; the meek because they "shall inherit the earth"; those who hunger because they "shall be satisfied"; the merciful because they "shall obtain mercy"; the pure in heart because they "shall see God"; the peacemakers because they "shall be called sons of God"; and finally those who are persecuted for righteousness because "theirs is the kingdom of heaven."

The major difficulty in understanding the beatitudes, which is also true for faith in general, is due to the disappearance of the concept of eternity from our horizon. Marxist suspicion first came down on the word *eternity* because, according to that view, it draws people away from their historical duty to transform the world and to improve the present life; it leads to an avoidance of reality. Widespread materialism and consumerism have done the rest, making it even seem strange and almost inappropriate that, as time goes on, "modern" people still speak about eternity.

Nevertheless, despite its banishment into oblivion, there still remains a secret longing for eternity in everyone. A human being, the philosophers say, is a finite being capable of infinity, and precisely because of this capacity for infinity, people desire it and need it.

Some nonbelievers maintain that it is presumptuous to expect eternal life. They say that we need to be content with this life and peacefully leave the world to our children and to those who will come after us. I do not doubt their sincerity, but I have difficulty believing that this kind of thinking leaves them truly happy and satisfied. The philosopher Miguel de Unamuno (who was a secular thinker) responded this way to a friend who reproved him for being proud and presumptuous because of his quest for eternity:

> I am not saying that we deserve an afterlife or that logic demonstrates it; I am saying that we need it, whether we

deserve it or not, and that's all. I am saying that what passes away does not satisfy me, that I long for eternity, and that without it everything is indifferent to me. Without eternity there is no longer any joy in living.... It is very easy to say, "Get on with your life; you need to be satisfied with this life." But what about those who are not satisfied with that?[28]

No one who desires eternity, he says, exhibits a lack of love for life. The one who does not love life is the one who does not desire eternity, since that person is so easily resigned to the idea that life should end. Saint Augustine expressed the same idea when he wrote, "For to whomsoever eternal life is not given, of what benefit is...living well?"[29] If eternity is denied to people, then they will suddenly exclaim, as Macbeth did after killing the king,

> There is nothing serious in mortality:
> All is but toys. Renown and grace is dead,
> The wine of life is drawn.[30]

Every year there is a national meeting in Rimini of the charismatic renewal, to which I am often invited to speak. One year I felt inspired to speak about eternity, and I believe I did so with great conviction and enthusiasm. I wanted to revive that defunct word, and every so often I invited the crowd (more than fifty thousand people) to repeat with me, "Eternity! Eternity!" It was like being on Christopher Columbus's ship when—after all hope had been lost—they heard the sentinel cry out one morning, "Land! Land!"

The enthusiasm was so great that later on someone printed up some bumper stickers for cars. On one there was an "I" with a red heart, meaning "I love," followed by the word "eternity." On another was a verse from a believing poet: "Everything in the world, except eternity, is vain."[31]

It is true that "the truth of the beatitudes has not yet found a place in the earth," at least not as we would like, but Jesus did not proclaim them in vain if, while we are still living in time, they help us to keep alive that longing for eternity.

AN EXAMINATION OF CONSCIENCE BASED
ON THE BEATITUDES

The best way to take the Gospel beatitudes seriously is to use them as a mirror for an examination of conscience that is truly "evangelical." All of Scripture, says Saint James, is like a mirror into which the believer should gaze calmly and without haste in order to know what he or she is truly like (see James 1:23–25), but the beatitudes provide a unique mirror.

Blessed are the poor in spirit, for theirs is the kingdom of heaven. Am I poor in spirit, poor within, having abandoned everything to God? Am I free and detached from earthly goods? What does money mean to me? Do I seek to lead a sober and simple lifestyle that is fitting for someone who wants to bear witness to the gospel? Do I take to heart the problem of the terrible poverty that is not chosen but imposed on so many millions of my brothers and sisters?

Blessed are those who mourn, for they shall be comforted. Do I consider affliction a misfortune and a punishment, as some people in the world do, or as an opportunity to be like Christ? What are the reasons when I am sad: the same as God's or the same as the world's? Do I seek to console others or only to be consoled myself? Do I know how to keep an adversity a secret between God and me, not talking about it every chance I get?

Blessed are the meek, for they shall inherit the earth. Am I meek? There is a violence of action but also a violence of speech and thought. Do I control anger outside of and within me? Am I kind and friendly to those around me?

Blessed are those who hunger and thirst for righteousness, for they shall be satisfied. Do I hunger and thirst for holiness? Do I strive for holiness, or am I at times satisfied with mediocrity and lukewarmness? Does the physical hunger of millions of people lead me to question my continual search for comfort, my middle-class lifestyle? Do I realize how much I and the world in which I live resemble the rich man who feasted daily?

Blessed are the merciful, for they shall obtain mercy. Am I merciful? When a brother, a sister or a coworker demonstrates a fault, do I react with judgment or with mercy? Jesus felt compassion for the crowd; do I? Have I at times been the servant who was forgiven but does not forgive others? How many times have I casually asked for and received the mercy of God for my sins without taking into account the price that Christ paid for me to receive it?

Blessed are the pure in heart, for they shall see God. Am I pure of heart? Are my intentions pure? Do I say yes and no as Jesus did? There is a purity of heart, a purity of lips, a purity of eyes, a purity of body: Do I seek to cultivate all these kinds of purity that are so necessary—especially to consecrated souls? The clearest opposite of purity of heart is hypocrisy. Whom do I seek to please by my actions: God or other people?

Blessed are the peacemakers, for they shall be called sons of God. Am I a peacemaker? Do I bring peace to different sides? How do I behave when there are conflicts of opinion or conflicts of interest? Do I strive always to report only good things, positive words, and strive to let evil things, gossip and whatever might sow dissension, fall on deaf ears? Is the peace of God in my heart, and if not, why not?

Blessed are those who are persecuted for righteousness' sake, for theirs is the kingdom of heaven. Am I ready to suffer in silence for the gospel? How do I react when facing a wrong or an injury I have received? Do I participate intimately in the suffering of brothers and sisters who truly suffer for their faith or for social justice and freedom?

$\mathcal{N}otes$

PREFACE

1. Gregory the Great, *Morals on the Book of Job*, 20, 1 (Oxford: John Henry Parker, 1845), p. 446.

CHAPTER ONE: BLESSED ARE THE POOR IN SPIRIT, FOR THEIRS IS THE
KINGDOM OF HEAVEN

1. The *am ha'aretz*, the "people of the land," were common people.

2. See Albert Gelin, *The Poor of Yahweh*, Kathryn Sullivan, trans. (Collegeville, Minn.: Liturgical, 1964), especially pp. 18–26; Albert Gelin, *Les pauvres que Dieu aime* [The Poor Whom God Loves] (Paris: Les Editions du Cerf, 1968).

3. Augustine, "Sermon 3," 1 ["Sermon 53," 1 in *PL* 38, 365], J.G. Cunningham, trans., vol. 1, *Nicene and Post-Nicene Fathers*, Philip Schaff, ed. (Grand Rapids: Eerdmans, 1956), p. 266; see also Leo the Great, "Sermon 95," 2–3, Charles Lett Feltoe, trans., vol. 12, *Nicene and Post-Nicene Fathers*, Philip Schaff and Henry Wace, eds. (New York: Christian Literature, 1895), p. 203.

4. See Jacques Dupont, *Les béatitudes*, 3 vols. (Paris: J. Gabalda, 1969–1973).

5. Thomas Aquinas, *Summa theologica*, III, q. 40, a. 3, Fathers of the English Dominican Province, trans. (Westminster, Md.: Christian Classics, 1981), vol. 4, p. 2232.

6. Angela of Foligno, *Instructions*, in *Angela of Foligno: Complete Works*, Paul Lachance, trans. (New York: Paulist, 1993), pp. 303–304.

7. Gregory of Nyssa, *The Beatitudes*, 1, Hilda C. Graef, trans., vol. 18, *Ancient Christian Writers*, Johannes Quaesten and Joseph C. Plumpe, eds. (Westminster, Md.: Newman, 1954), p. 91.

8. See Giuseppe Visonà, Enrico dal Covolo, Felice Cesano, eds., "*Per foramen acus: Il cristianesimo antico di fronte alla pericope evangelica del giovane ricco*" [Ancient Christianity on the Gospel Pericope of the Rich Young Man], *Studia Patristica Mediolanensia*, 14 (Milan:Vita e Pensiero, 1986).

9. Clement of Alexandria, "Who Is the Rich Man That Shall Be Saved?" William Wilson, trans., vol. 2, *The Ante-Nicene Fathers*, Alexander Roberts and James Donaldson, eds. (New York: Charles Scribner's Sons, 1926), p. 595.

10. *Lumen Gentium*, Dogmatic Constitution on the Church, 8, in *Vatican Council II: The Conciliar and Post Conciliar Documents*, Austin Flannery, ed. (Northport, N.Y.: Costello, 1998), pp. 357–358.

11. See Augustine, *Homilies on the Gospel of John*, 32, 8, John Gibb and James Innes, trans., vol. 7, *Nicene and Post-Nicene Fathers*, Philip Schaff, ed. (Grand Rapids: Eerdmans, 1956), p. 195.

12. Francis of Assisi, *The Mirror of Perfection*, 12, in *The Little Flowers of St. Francis; The Mirror of Perfection; The Life of St. Francis*, Robert Steele, trans. (New York: Dutton, 1910), p. 195.

13. Jerome K. Jerome, *Three Men in a Boat: To Say Nothing of the Dog* (New York: Time-Life Books, 1964), pp. 24–25.

CHAPTER TWO: BLESSED ARE YOU THAT WEEP NOW, FOR YOU SHALL LAUGH

1. Charles Péguy, *The Portico of the Mystery of the Second Virtue*, Dorothy Brown Aspinwall, trans. (Metuchen, N.J.: Scarecrow, 1970), pp. 68–70.

2. Lucretius, *The Nature of Things*, 4, 1113–1114 [*De Rerum Natura*, 4, 1129–1130], A.E. Stallings, trans. (New York: Penguin, 2007), p. 141.

3. Charles Baudelaire, *The Flowers of Evil*, Keith Waldrop, trans. (Middleton, Conn.: Wesleyan University Press, 2006), passim.

4. Maximos [sic] the Confessor, *Four Hundred Texts on Love, Fourth Century*, 39, in *Philokalia*, G.E.H. Palmer et al., trans., vol. 2 (Boston: Faber & Faber, 1981), p. 245.

5. See Dupont, vol. 3, pp. 545–555.

6. Virgil, *The Aeneid*, 1, 628–629 [1, 462, in the original], Robert Fitzgerald, trans. (New York: Vintage, 1990), p. 20.

7. Michel Onfray, *Atheist Manifesto: The Case Against Christianity, Judaism, and Islam*, Jeremy Leggatt, trans. (New York: Arcade, 2005).

8. Richard Dawkins, *The God Delusion* (New York: Bantam, 2006).

9. Sam Harris, *The End of Faith: Religion, Terror, and the Future of Reason* (New York: Norton, 2004).
10. Telmo Pievani, *Creazione senza Dio* (Turin: Enaudi, 2006).
11. Eugenio Lecaldano, *Un' etica senza Dio* (Bari: Laterza, 2006).
12. Christopher Hitchens, *God Is Not Great: How Religion Poisons Everything* (New York: Hachette, 2007).
13. Carlo Augusto Viano, *Laici in ginocchio* [Skeptics on Their Knees] (Bari: Laterza, 2006).
14. Gotthold Lessing, "On the Proof of the Spirit and of Power," in *Lessing's Theological Writings*, Henry Chadwick, trans. (Stanford, Calif.: Stanford University Press, 1957), pp. 51–52.
15. Søren Kierkegaard, *The Sickness unto Death*, in *The Essential Kierkegaard*, Howard V. Hong and Edna H. Hong, eds. (Princeton, N.J.: Princeton University Press, 1995), pp. 140–141.
16. Benedict XVI, Address to the Irish Bishops on their *Ad Limina* Visit, Saturday, October 28, 2006, available at: www.vatican.va.
17. Augustine, *The Confessions of St. Augustine*, bk. 10, chap. 43, John K. Ryan, trans. (Garden City, N.Y.: Image, 1960), p. 274.
18. Douglas Groothius, *On Pascal* (Belmont, Calif.: Wadsworth, 2003), p. 13.
19. Symeon the New Theologian, "Discourse 35," 11 ("In the Form of a Thanksgiving"), in *Symeon the New Theologian: The Discourses*, C.J. deCatanzaro, trans. (New York: Paulist, 1980), p. 376.
20. Symeon the New Theologian, "Tenth Ethical Discourse," in *On the Mystical Life: The Ethical Discourses*, Alexander Golitzin, trans., vol. 1 (Crestwood, N.Y.: St. Vladimir's Seminary Press, 1995), p. 167.
21. Symeon the New Theologian, "Discourse 35," 10, p. 375.

CHAPTER THREE: BLESSED ARE THE MEEK, FOR THEY SHALL INHERIT THE EARTH

1. French does not have a specific word for "meek." In *Dictionnaire de spiritualité ascétique et mystique, doctrine et histoire* [Dictionary of Ascetic and Mystical Spirituality, Doctrine and History], vol. 3, Charles Baumgartner et al., eds. (Paris: Beauchesne, 1967), this virtue is treated under the heading of *douceur*, "sweetness" (pp. 674–676).

2. Augustine, "Sermon 14," in *Sermons 1–19*, Edmund Hill, trans., part 3, vol. 1, *The Works of Saint Augustine*, John E. Rotelle, ed. (Brooklyn: New City, 1990), p. 321.

3. Thomas Aquinas, I–II, q. 69, a. 1, vol. 2, pp. 885–886.

4. Thomas Aquinas, I–II, q. 106, a. 2, vol. 2, p. 1105.

5. Gerd Theissen and Annette Merz, *The Historical Jesus: A Comprehensive Guide* (Minneapolis: Fortress, 1998), pp. 397–398.

6. Mahatma K. Gandhi, *All Religions Are True*, Anand T. Hingorani, ed. (Mumbai: Bharatiya Vidya Bhavan, 1962), p. 56.

7. See Augustine, *Confessions*, bk. 10, chap. 43, p. 274.

8. Friedrich Nietzsche, *Beyond Good and Evil*, 9, 260, Helen Zimmern, trans., *The Philosophy of Nietzsche* (New York: Modern Library, 1954), pp. 578–582.

9. Friedrich Nietzsche, *The Will to Power*, 4, 1052, Walter Kaufmann and R.J. Hollingdale, trans. (New York: Vintage, 1967), pp. 542–543.

10. René Girard, *I See Satan Fall Like Lightning*, James G. Williams, trans. (Maryknoll, N.Y.: Orbis, 2001), p. 164. "Mimetic desire" is the desire to be like one's neighbor and to have what one's neighbor has; Girard connects it to the tenth commandment.

11. See especially chapter thirteen, "The Modern Concern for Victims," in Girard, pp. 161–169.

12. In the *Revised Standard Version*, Catholic Edition (Ignatius), these verses are in the footnote for Luke 9:55.

13. See Augustine, "Letter 93," 5, 17, J.G. Cunningham, trans., vol. 1, *Nicene and Post-Nicene Fathers*: "For originally my opinion was, that no one should be coerced into the unity of Christ, that we must act only by words, fight only by arguments, and prevail by force of reason" (p. 388).

14. See Augustine, vol. 1, *Nicene and Post-Nicene Fathers*, "Letter 173," 10, pp. 546–547; "Letter 208," 7, pp. 559–560.

15. Corrado Augias and Mauro Pesce, *Inchiesta su Gesù: Chi era l'uomo che ha cambiato il mondo* [The Jesus Inquest: Revealing the Man Who Changed the World] (Milan: Mondadori, 2006), p. 52.

16. Giovanni Papini (1881–1956), a controversial, anti-traditional Italian essayist, critic, poet and novelist who began as an atheist and ended as a spokesman for Roman Catholicism.

17. Ignatius of Antioch, "Letter to the Ephesians," 10, 2, Francis X. Glimm, trans., vol. 1, *The Fathers of the Church*, Bernard M. Peebles, ed. (Washington, D.C.: Catholic University of America Press, 1947), p. 91.

18. Francis de Sales, *The Spiritual Maxims of St. Francis de Sales*, C.F. Kelley, ed. (New York: Harper and Brothers, 1953), p. 99.

19. Augustine, *Homilies on 1 John*, 7, 8, in *Augustine: Later Works*, John Burnaby, trans. (Philadelphia: Westminster, 1955), p. 316.

20. See Augustine, *Confessions*, bk. 10, chap. 29, p. 256.

CHAPTER FOUR: BLESSED ARE YOU WHO HUNGER NOW, FOR YOU SHALL BE SATISFIED

1. C.H. Dodd, *History and Gospel*, rev. ed. (London: Hodder and Stoughton, 1964), p. 20.

2. Henri de Lubac, *Medieval Exegesis*, Mark Sebanc, trans., vol. 1 (Grand Rapids: Eerdmans, 1998), p. 79.

3. John Paul II, *Sollicitudo Rei Socialis* [On Social Concern], 42 (Boston: St. Paul, 1988), p. 80.

4. Benedict XVI, Address to the Diplomatic Corps at the Holy See, January 8, 2007, available at: www.vatican.va.

5. See Dupont, vol. 3, p. 355.

6. Adolf von Harnack and Wilhelm Herrmann, *Essays on the Social Gospel*, G.M. Craik, trans., Maurice A. Canney, ed. (New York: Putnam, 1907), p. 11.

7. Rudolf Bultmann, *Primitive Christianity in Its Contemporary Setting*, R.H. Fuller, trans. (New York: Meridian, 1956), p. 206.

8. Pope Benedict XVI, *The Sacrament of Charity* [*Sacramentum caritatis*], 90 (Washington, D.C.: United States Conference of Catholic Bishops, 2007), p. 76. This apostolic exhortation was delivered on the Feast of the Chair of Peter, February 22, 2007.

CHAPTER FIVE: BLESSED ARE THE MERCIFUL, FOR THEY SHALL OBTAIN MERCY

1. E.P. Sanders, *Jesus and Judaism* (Philadelphia: Fortress, 1985), p. 385, note 14.

2. James D. G. Dunn, *Jesus Remembered*, vol. 1, *Christianity in the Making* (Grand Rapids: Eerdmans, 2003), p. 532.

3. Péguy, p. 91.

4. Fyodor Dostoevsky, *The Idiot*, Henry Carlisle and Olga Carlisle, trans. (New York: New American Library, 1969), p. 240.

5. Franz Kafka, *The Trial*, Willa Muir and Edwin Muir, trans. (New York: The Modern Library, 1956), p. 198.

6. Francis Xavier Van Thuan, *Testimony of Hope*, Julia Mary Darrenkamp and Anne Eileen Heffernan, trans. (Boston: Pauline, 2000), p. 38.

7. Augustine, *"Lutea vasa quae faciunt invicem angustias:"* "Sermon 69," 1, Edmund Hill, trans., part 3, in vol. 3, *The Works of Saint Augustine*, John E. Rotelle, ed. (Brooklyn: New City, 1991), p. 235.

8. Péguy, p. 8.

9. See, for example, Dalai Lama, Tenzin Gyatso, *Ethics for a New Millennium* (New York: Riverhead, 1999).

CHAPTER SIX: BLESSED ARE THE PURE IN HEART, FOR THEY SHALL SEE GOD

1. Although not said by Augustine, this phrase is often used to summarize his commentary on pagan virtues in *The City of God*, 19, 25.

2. Augustine, *Our Lord's Sermon on the Mount*, 2, 1, 1, S.D.F. Salmond, trans., vol. 6, *Nicene and Post-Nicene Fathers*, Philip Schaff, ed. (Grand Rapids: Eerdmans, 1956), p. 34.

3. Augustine, *Our Lord's Sermon on the Mount*, 2, 13, 45–46, p. 48.

4. Gregory of Nyssa, *The Beatitudes*, 6, p. 149.

5. See Basil the Great, *On the Holy Spirit*, 9, 23, George Lewis, trans. (London: Religious Tract Society, 1888), pp. 22, 53–54, 106–107.

6. See Michel Dupuy, "Pureté, purification," 1–2, in *Dictionnaire de spiritualité ascétique et mystique, doctrine et histoire*, vol. 12, Marcel Viller et al., eds. (Paris: Beauchesne, 1986), part 2, cols. 2637–2645.

7. Bernard of Clairvaux, *Sentences* 3, 2, Francis R. Swietek, trans., in *The Parables and Sentences*, Maureen M. O'Brien, ed. (Kalamazoo, Mich.: Cistercian, 2000), pp. 187–188.

8. John Chrysostom, *Homilies on the Gospel of Saint Matthew*, 15, 6, trans. George Prevost, vol. 10, *Nicene and Post-Nicene Fathers*, Philip Schaff, ed. (Grand Rapids: Eerdmans, 1956), p. 94.

9. John Ruusbroec, *"The Spiritual Espousals" and Other Works*, James A. Wiseman, trans. (New York: Paulist, 1985), p. 64.

10. Blaise Pascal, *Pensées*, 147, 153, W.F. Trotter, trans. (Franklin, Pa.: Franklin Library, 1979), pp. 47–48.

11. Augustine, *Our Lord's Sermon on the Mount*, 2, 2, 5, p. 35.

12. See, for example, Jean Baudrillard, "Virtuality and Events," in *The Intelligence of Evil or the Lucidity Pact*, Chris Turner, trans. (New York: Berg, 2005), pp. 117–138.

13. Kierkegaard, C, 11, 191, p. 363.

14. Francis of Assisi, *Admonitions*, 12, 2, in *Francis and Clare: The Complete Works*, Regis J. Armstrong and Ignatius Brady, trans. (New York: Paulist, 1982), p. 33.

15. See Adrian Michaels, "Naked Ambition," *Financial Times*, July 14, 2007. Michaels is the *Financial Times* correspondent in Milan.

16. Gabriella Jacomella, "L'Italia è il paese delle donne nude" ["Italy, the Country of Nude Women"], *Corriere dell Sera*, July 15, 2007.

17. See Hermann L. Strack and Paul Billerbeck, *Das Evangelium nach Matthäus* [The Gospel According to Matthew], vol. 1 (Munich: C. H. Beck'sche Verlagsbuchhandlung, 1926), p. 718.

18. Augustine, *Confessions*, bk. 10, chap. 36, no. 59, p. 267.

19. Lauretta, *Il bosco dei lillà* [The Forest of Lilacs] (Milan: Ancora, 1994), p. 90.

CHAPTER SEVEN: BLESSED ARE THE PEACEMAKERS, FOR THEY SHALL BE CALLED SONS OF GOD

1. Dupont, vol. 3, p. 637.

2. This meditation was given to the papal household during Advent 2006.

3. Benedict XVI, "The Human Person, the Heart of Peace," 3, Message for the World Day of Peace, January 1, 2007, available at: www.vatican.va, emphasis in original.

4. See Nicholas Zernov, *The Russians and Their Church*, 3rd ed. (Crestwood, N.Y.: St. Vladimir's Seminary Press, 1994), p. 41.

5. See Dionysius the Areopagite, *On the Divine Names*, 11, 1–6, in *On the Divine Names and the Mystical Theology*, C.E. Rolt, trans. (New York: Macmillan, 1920), pp. 173–180.

6. Augustine, *The City of God*, 19, 13, Gerald G. Walsh et al., trans. (New York: Image, 1958), p. 456.

7. Thomas Aquinas, *Commentary on the Gospel of John*, 14, 7, n. 1962.

8. Dante Alighieri, *Paradiso*, 3.85, *The Divine Comedy*, Mark Musa, trans., vol. 3, rev. ed. (New York: Penguin, 1986), p. 35.

9. Teresa of Avila, "Poem 9," in *The Complete Works of St. Teresa of Jesus*, E. Allison Peers, trans., vol. 3 (London: Sheed and Ward, 1946), p. 288.

10. See Hans Küng, "Preface," *Tracing the Way: Spiritual Dimensions of the World Religions*, John Bowden, trans. (New York: Continuum, 2002), p. xv.

11. Benedict XVI, as quoted in John Thavis, "In Sign of Respect to Muslims, Pope Prays in Istanbul's Blue Mosque," *Catholic News Service*, November 30, 2006.

12. Thomas Aquinas, I–II, q. 109, a. 1, vol. 2, p. 1124; Ambrosiaster, *Commentary on 1 Corinthians* 12, 3, *Corpus Scriptorum ecclesiasticorum latinorum* 81, p. 132.

13. John Lennon, as quoted in Geoffrey Giuliano, *Lennon in America* (New York: Cooper Square, 2000), p. 24.

14. Girard, pp. 10–11; see chap. 3, fn. 10, on "mimetic desire."

15. Jean-Paul Sartre, "The Devil & the Good Lord," 3, 10, Kitty Black, trans., in *The Devil & the Good Lord, and Two Other Plays* (New York: Alfred A. Knopf, 1960), p. 142.

16. Jean-Paul Sartre, "No Exit" [*Huis Clos*], sc. 5, in *"No Exit" and Three Other Plays* (New York: Vintage, 1955), p. 47.

17. Benedict XVI, "The Human Person, the Heart of Peace," no. 5, emphasis in the original.

18. The Holy Qur'an, sura 3, 45–47 (993), Abdullah Ysuf Ali, rev. and trans. (Brentwood, Md.: Amana, 1993), p. 139.

19. Magdi Allam, "Noi musulmani diciamo sì al presepe" ["We Muslims Say Yes to the Manger"], *Corriere della Sera*, December 18, 2006, p. 18.

20. Leo the Great, *Tractates*, 26, *Corpus Christianorum Series Latina* 138, line 130.

21. *Idiomelon*, Christmas Vespers.

CHAPTER EIGHT: BLESSED ARE THOSE WHO ARE PERSECUTED FOR
RIGHTEOUSNESS' SAKE, FOR THEIRS IS THE KINGDOM OF HEAVEN

1. Benedict XVI, "The Human Person, the Heart of Peace," no. 5.

2. Following the original publication of this book in Italian, during the Easter Mass at St. Peter's Basilica in 2008, Magdi Allam became a Roman Catholic.

3. Heinrich Schlier, *Principalities and Powers in the New Testament* (New York: Herder and Herder, 1961), pp. 31–32.

4. Hitchens, p. 12, emphasis in original.

5. See various apologies like *De fuga sua* by Athanasius and *De fuga persecutione* by Tertullian.

6. *Chronicles of the Twenty-four Generals of the Order of Friars Minor*, vol. 3, *Analecta Franciscana* (Quarrachi: ex Typographia Collegii S. Bonaventurae, 1885–1941), pp. 15–19.

7. Francis of Assisi, "The Earlier Rule" ["Regula non bullata"], 16, in Armstrong and Brady, p. 121, emphasis in original.

8. Augustine, "Letter 89," 2, in vol. 1, *Nicene and Post-Nicene Fathers*, p. 374; *Against Cresconius*, 3, 47, 51: "*Non poena sed causa facit martyres.*"

9. See Augustine, *Homilies on the Gospel of John*, 6, 23: "It was by charity those martyrs.... suffered in time of persecution" (p. 47).

10. Bernado Olivera, *How Far to Follow? The Martyrs of Atlas* (Kalamazoo, Mich.: Cistercian, 1997), p. 96.

11. Olivera, p. 97.

12. Olivera, pp. 97–98.

13. Augustine, "Sermon 335 H," 2, Edmund Hill, trans., part 3, vol. 9, *The Works of Saint Augustine*, John Rotelle, ed. (Hyde Park, N.Y.: New City, 1994), p. 247.

14. Horace, "*Si fractus illabatur orbis / impavidum ferient ruinae*" ["If the heavens crack / And fall, he'll cooly let the ruin rain"], *The Odes of Horace*, III, 3, l. 7–8, James Michie, trans. (New York: Washington Square, 1965), p. 132 (Latin), p. 133 (English).

15. See this story in Ambrose, *De officiis*, 1, 41, Ivor J. Davidson, trans., vol. 1 (New York: Oxford University Press, 2001), p. 239.

16. Legendary Roman hero who placed his right hand in the fire to show contempt for his Etruscan captors who had condemned him to be burned.

17. Georges Bernanos, "Dialogues of the Carmelites" [*Dialogues avec les Carmélites*], Michael Legat, trans., in *The Heroic Faces of Innocence: Three Stories by Georges Bernanos* (Grand Rapids: Eerdmans, 1999).

18. Gertrud von le Fort, *The Song at the Scaffold: A Novel of Horror and Holiness in the Reign of Terror*, Olga Marx, trans. (New York: Sheed

and Ward, 1933).

19. T.S. Eliot, *Murder in the Cathedral*, Part 1, in *Collected Plays* (London: Faber and Faber, 1962), p. 27.

20. Eliot, "Interlude," p. 33.

21. Dupont, vol. 3, pp. 334–340.

22. Clement of Rome, "Second Letter to the Corinthians," 13, 3, in *The Apostolic Fathers*, Francis X. Glimm et al., trans. (Washington, D.C.: Catholic University of America Press, 1947), p. 73.

23. Søren Kierkegaard, *The Gospel of Suffering*, 4, in *The Gospel of Suffering and the Lilies of the Field*, David F. Swenson and Lillian Marvin Swenson, trans. (Minneapolis: Augsburg, 1948), p. 76.

24. "Epistle to Diognetus," 5, 11, in *Ancient Christian Writers*, vol. 6, Johannes Quasten and Joseph L. Plumpe, eds. (New York: Paulist, 1948), p. 139.

25. Erri De Luca and Gennaro Matino, *Sottosopra* [Upside Down] (Milan: Mondadori, 2007), p. 21.

26. Thomas Aquinas, I–II, q. 69, a. 2, vol. 1, p. 887.

27. Charles Péguy, *The Mystery of the Charity of Joan of Arc*, Julian Green, trans. (New York: Pantheon, 1950), pp. 10–11.

28. Miguel de Unamuno, "Cartas inéditas de Miguel de Unamuno y Pedro Jiménez Ilundain," Hernán Benítez, ed. *Revista de la Universidad de Buenos Aires*, vol. 3, no. 9 (January–March 1949), pp. 135, 150.

29. Augustine, *Homilies on the Gospel of John*, 45, 2, p. 250.

30. William Shakespeare, "Macbeth," Act 2, scene 3, 93–95, in *The Complete Signet Classic Shakespeare*, Sylvan Barnet, ed. (New York: Harcourt Brace Jovanovich, 1963), p. 1242.

31. Antonio Fogazzaro, "A Sera," in *Le poesie* (Milan: Mondadori, 1935), pp. 194–197: "Tutto, Signore / Tranne l'Eterno, al mondo / È vano" (l. 21–23).